Administrative Law

BLACK LETTER OUTLINES

Administrative Law

by Russell L. Weaver

Professor of Law & Distinguished University Scholar
University of Louisville
Louis D. Brandeis School of Law

William D. Araiza

Professor of Law
Brooklyn Law School

SECOND EDITION

WEST®

Mat #40859072

Black Letter Series is a trademark registered in the U.S. Patent and Trademark Office.

© West, a Thomson business, 2006
© 2013 LEG, Inc. d/b/a West Academic Publishing
   610 Opperman Drive
   St. Paul, MN 55123
   1–800–313–9378

West, West Academic Publishing, and West Academic are trademarks of West Publishing Corporation, used under license.

Printed in the United States of America

ISBN: 978–0–314–90408–9

Dedication

To Ben and Kate, with love, RLW

To Stephen, WDA

*

Summary of Contents

■ CHAPTER ONE: RULEMAKING

■ CHAPTER TWO: ADJUDICATIONS

■ CHAPTER THREE: CHOICE OF PROCEDURES AND NON–LEGISLATIVE RULES

■ CHAPTER FOUR: THE AVAILABILITY OF JUDICIAL REVIEW

■ CHAPTER FIVE: INSPECTIONS, REPORTS & SUBPOENAS

■ CHAPTER SIX: AGENCY STRUCTURE

■ CHAPTER SEVEN: PUBLIC ACCESS TO AGENCY PROCESSES

■ CHAPTER EIGHT: ATTORNEY'S FEES

APPENDICES

App.

Table of Contents

■ CHAPTER ONE: RULEMAKING

■ CHAPTER TWO: ADJUDICATIONS

■ CHAPTER THREE: CHOICE OF PROCEDURES AND NON–LEGISLATIVE RULES

■ CHAPTER FOUR: THE AVAILABILITY OF JUDICIAL REVIEW

■ CHAPTER FIVE: INSPECTIONS, REPORTS & SUBPOENAS

■ CHAPTER SIX: AGENCY STRUCTURE

■ CHAPTER SEVEN: PUBLIC ACCESS TO AGENCY PROCESSES

■ CHAPTER EIGHT: ATTORNEY'S FEES

APPENDICES

App.

Capsule Summary

■ CHAPTER ONE: RULEMAKING

A. THE RULEMAKING PROCESS

Agencies usually have two options for making rules: formal rulemaking processes (the equivalent of trial-type procedures) & informal rulemaking procedures (which utilize so-called "notice and comment" procedures). Some statutes may also impose "hybrid" procedures, which involve a cross between formal and informal rulemaking procedures.

B. RULEMAKING INITIATION

An agency may decide to initiate a rulemaking on its own motion. Alternatively, an agency may be commanded to do so by Congress, or interested parties may petition for a rulemaking under Section 553(e).

C. EXEMPTIONS FROM RULEMAKING

Section 553 of the APA governs rulemaking and provides for informal rulemaking by "notice and comment" procedures, and formal rulemaking (trial-type proceedings) under sections 556 and 557. Under APA Section 553, various types of rules are exempt either from the entire rulemaking procedure, or from one or more of that procedure's components.

D. TYPES OF RULEMAKING PROCESSES

Rulemaking processes can be described as informal, formal, and hybrid. Although the APA only provides for formal and informal rulemaking processes, Congress sometimes imposes additional requirements (hybrid procedures) in addition to or in place of notice and comment procedures.

E. INFORMAL RULEMAKING

Informal rulemaking, also referred to as "notice and comment rulemaking," requires the agency to provide notice in the *Federal Register* to institute rulemaking, and requires that agencies give persons a chance to submit written comments on the proposed rule. 5 U.S.C.A. § 553. Congress rarely requires agencies to utilize formal rulemaking procedures, provided for in APA sections 556–57, which essentially require agencies to create rules using trial-type procedures.

1. Choice Between Formal and Informal Procedures

In general, agencies use "informal" rather than "formal" rulemaking procedures, and neither Congress nor the courts require agencies to use formal procedures. In most cases courts will require agencies to engage in formal rulemaking only when Congress explicitly requires that the agency act "on the record after opportunity for agency hearing."

2. Notice Requirements for Informal Rulemaking

a. Notice and Changes in a Rule's Text

Courts have held that a Notice of Proposed Rulemaking (NOPR) must "fairly apprise interested persons" of the issues in the rulemaking. If the final rule is not a "logical outgrowth" of the original notice, the agency must issue a new NOPR.

3. Opportunity for Comment

APA Section 553(c) requires agencies to provide interested persons with an opportunity to comment on NOPRs by the "submission of written data, views, or arguments." In recent years agencies have made it possible for comments to be submitted online, via regulations.gov.

a. *Ex Parte* Communications

Outside contacts are normally permitted during the rulemaking process, except when the rulemaking involves "competing private claims to a valuable privilege." *Sangamon Valley Television Corp. v. United States*, 269 F.2d 221 (D.C. Cir. 1959) (holding that due process prohibits such contacts when the rulemaking concerns such competing claims).

4. Statement of Basis and Purpose

After receiving comments from interested persons, Section 553(c) requires agencies "after consideration of the relevant matter presented, [to] incorporate in the rules adopted a concise general statement of their basis and purpose."

F. HYBRID RULEMAKING PROCEDURES

In some instances, agencies issue rules using "hybrid" procedures—essentially a combination of informal and formal rulemaking procedures. In some instances, agencies choose to use hybrid procedures. In other instances, Congress mandates that agencies include additional procedures in addition to APA–mandated procedures. In *Vermont Yankee Nuclear Power Corp. v. Natural Resources Defense Council, Inc.* 435 U.S. 519, 98 S.Ct. 1197, 55 L.Ed.2d 460 (1978), the Court held that courts could not impose hybrid rulemaking procedures on an agency. However, Congress can always supersede or supplement the APA's requirements and impose additional or unique procedural requirements for a particular rulemaking. In addition, since 1981 presidents have required review of at least some agency rules through the White House Office of Management and Budget (OMB).

G. STATE RULEMAKING PROCEDURES

Most states tend to use informal, notice-and-comment, rulemaking processes. However, some states have imposed hybrid requirements.

H. NEGOTIATED RULEMAKING

In recent years, there has been a movement to implement so-called "negotiated rulemaking." The hope is that through negotiation, as opposed to adversarial relationships, the parties can cooperate to reach creative solutions to problems. If they succeed, the negotiated rule is then formalized through the ordinary rulemaking process.

I. JUDICIAL REVIEW OF RULES

When agencies issue rules, courts are free to substantively review the results of those rules on the basis that the rule is inconsistent with the agency's governing statute, or that the rule itself is arbitrary and capricious.

1. Statutory Interpretation

Section 706 of the APA directs reviewing courts to hold unlawful agency action "not in accordance with law," 5 U.S.C.A. § 706(2)(A), and agency action "in excess of statutory jurisdiction, authority, limitations, or short of statutory right," *id.* § 706(2)(C).

a. *Chevron* Deference

In *Chevron U.S.A., Inc. v. Natural Resources Defense Council, Inc.*, 467 U.S. 837, 104 S.Ct. 2778, 81 L.Ed.2d 694 (1984), the Court suggested that reviewing courts should be deferential to agency-issued rules. When the meaning of a statute is unclear, a reasonable interpretation is entitled to deference. Sometimes, instead of *Chevron* deference, courts will review agency statutory interpretations under the deference standard enunciated in *Skidmore v. Swift & Co.*, 323 U.S. 134, 65 S.Ct. 161, 89 L.Ed. 124 (1944), which entails courts deferring based on the underlying merits of the agency's interpretive analysis.

2. Substantive Content of Rules

Section 706 provides that a "reviewing court shall . . . hold unlawful and set aside agency action, findings, and conclusions found to be—(A) arbitrary, capricious, an abuse of discretion or not otherwise in accordance with law; . . . [and] (E) unsupported by substantial evidence in a case subject to sections 556 and 557 of this title. . . . " 5 U.S.C.A. § 6706.

a. Scope of Review

Section 706 applies the "substantial evidence" test when agencies must create rules using formal procedures (trial-type procedures) under APA sections 556–557. By contrast, when an agency proceeds by notice and comment, the APA mandates application of the "arbitrary and capricious" standard. However, in some cases, Congress imposes a different standard of review.

b. "Substantial Evidence" Defined

The "substantial evidence" standard basically focuses on whether the record contains "such evidence as a reasonable mind might accept as adequate to support a conclusion."

c. **Arbitrary and Capricious Standard**

As the name suggests, the "arbitrary and capricious" standard requires courts to be deferential to agency action. Many believe that, in practice, there is little difference between the "arbitrary and capricious" and "substantial evidence" standards.

d. **Adequate Explanation**

In recent years, some courts have applied the arbitrary and capricious standard by inquiring whether there are "adequate reasons" supporting the agency's choices. At times this review has been searching, while at other times the review has been more deferential.

■ CHAPTER TWO: ADJUDICATIONS

A. INTRODUCTION

Adjudications and regulations are the two fundamentally different methods by which agencies impose legal obligations on private parties.

1. Adjudications Result in Orders

The APA defines adjudication as the "agency process for the formulation of an order." In turn, an order is defined as "the whole or part of any final disposition . . . in a matter other than rule making."

2. Rules Are Distinguished by Their Prospective Effect

A rule is defined as "the whole or a part of an agency statement of general or particular applicability and future effect designed to implement, interpret or prescribe law or policy . . . " Thus, adjudications are the process by which any final disposition other than one of future effect is reached.

3. The Rule/Order Distinction Tracks the Legislative/Judicial Distinction

In general, agency adjudications can be thought of as proceedings in which law is applied retrospectively to a party, just as in a normal court proceeding.

B. INFORMAL ADJUDICATION: INTRODUCTION

1. The Trigger for Formal Adjudication Is a Procedure Required to Be "On the Record After Opportunity for an Agency Hearing"

As described in the next section, the APA prescribes procedures for adjudications "required by statute to be determined on the record after opportunity for an agency hearing." 5 U.S.C. § 554(a).

2. Courts Sometimes Do Not Require Strict Adherence to This Language When Considering Whether Adjudications Have to Follow the APA's Formal Procedures

While courts in the rulemaking context have held that agencies need only satisfy the informal rulemaking procedures unless Congress uses exact words requiring more, courts are more willing to insist on formality in adjudication, since adjudication in general is thought of as a relatively formalized process.

3. The APA Requires No Particular Procedure for Informal Adjudications

When a court interprets the authorizing statute to not require formal adjudicatory procedures, the APA provides no guide as to what constitutes acceptable informal adjudication procedure.

4. In Cases of Informal Adjudication, the Due Process Clause Sets the Required Procedures

The lack of APA procedures for informal adjudications does not mean that in such situations agencies are completely free to use whatever procedures they wish (or none at all). Instead, if the Due Process clause of the Constitution applies, then it may mandate particular procedures.

C. WHEN THE DUE PROCESS CLAUSE IS TRIGGERED

The Due Process clause is generally thought to apply only to adjudications.

D. DUE PROCESS REQUIRES THREE INQUIRIES

Modern Due Process requires the following steps: determination that a life, liberty or property interest is at stake; a deprivation of that interest; and a determination of how much process is due before such a deprivation can take place.

E. THE EXISTENCE OF A DUE PROCESS INTEREST

1. Historically the Court Recognized Relatively Few Due Process—Protected Interests

Historically, only interests protectable at common law were recognized as protected interests. Such interests would include property and contract rights, and personal rights such as freedom to move about.

2. Modern Due Process Law Protects a Larger Number of Interests

In the late 1960's, the Court began to reconceptualize property and liberty to include not just common law-protected interests, but also interests that had been provided by statute, and upon which individuals could reasonably be expected to rely.

3. Modern Due Process Law Bases Its Analysis on Expectations

This new conception of property and liberty was based on the theory that the basic idea of property was grounded on individuals' reliance expectations, and that in the post-New Deal era individuals had come to expect not just protection of traditional property, but also the continuation of benefits that earlier doctrine had described as mere gratuities.

4. Under Modern Doctrine Licenses and Other Government Benefits Constitute Property

Under the modern rule, regulatory benefits such as licenses to practice law and veterans' benefits constitute property.

5. Due Process Interests Can Still Be Destroyed by Government Acting Against the Entire Class

Under the modern analysis, the legislature could destroy a property interest such as a veteran's benefit, by repealing the statute granting those benefits. However, it the government kept the benefit scheme in place but decided that a particular individual did not qualify, then that person would have a due process interest. In *Goldberg v. Kelly*, 397 U.S. 254, 90 S.Ct. 1011, 25 L.Ed.2d 287 (1970) the Court describes welfare benefits as due process-protected "property."

6. Liberty Interests Are Analyzed Similarly

This doctrine also applies to liberty interests, with the result that any governmental commitment to provide liberty would be held to engender reasonable expectations on the part of the beneficiary, and thus would be protected by due process.

7. Liberty Interests Can Also Be Found in the Due Process Clause's Liberty Prong Itself

In addition, more substantial liberty interests, *e.g.*, the right to marry, are protected independent of this analysis, by operation of the "liberty" component of the Due Process clause itself.

8. In Prison Contexts the Liberty Interest Must Be Significant in Itself in Order for Due Process to Apply

In *Sandin v. Conner*, 515 U.S. 472, 115 S.Ct. 2293, 132 L.Ed.2d 418 (1995), the Court stated that only "atypical and significant" deprivations beyond the confinement itself would count as due process protected interests.

F. DEPRIVATIONS MUST BE DELIBERATE

While "deprivation" might seem to connote any "impairment," the Supreme Court has ruled that a person is "deprived" of a due process protected interest only when the government has deliberately impaired that interest. Accidental government deprivations might give rise to a tort suit, but they do not implicate due process *per se*.

G. THE PROCESS THAT IS "DUE" IS BASED ON A BALANCING TEST

1. Expansion of the Interests Protected by Due Process Has Been Accompanied by a Reduction of the Process That Is Due

Assuming that government has deprived an individual of a due process protected interest, the question then arises whether the government has provided sufficient, or "due," process. In recent decades, as the Court has expanded the number of interests protected by due process, it has also reduced the amount of process that the Constitution requires.

2. The Court Employs a Balancing Test to Determine What Process Is Due

In *Mathews v. Eldridge*, 424 U.S. 319, 96 S.Ct. 893, 47 L.Ed.2d 18 (1976), the Court set forth a three part balancing test to determine how much process is due. The test requires a court to balance (1) the importance of the interest to the class of recipients; (2) the chance of erroneous deprivations under the current procedures and the increased accuracy the requested procedures would produce; and (3) the government's interest.

3. As Applied in *Mathews* Disability Benefits Were Not as Important as the Welfare Benefits in *Goldberg v. Kelly*

In *Mathews*, which dealt with a cut-off of social security disability benefits, with a hearing provided only after the benefits had been stopped, the Court noted that the benefits were not as important to the recipients as were the welfare payments in *Goldberg*, since welfare payments were predicated on a finding of need, unlike the disability payments.

4. The Nature of the Decision in *Mathews* Did Not Require an Oral Hearing to Improve Its Accuracy

With regard to the second factor, the *Mathews* Court noted that before the benefits cut off the beneficiary was afforded a chance to submit written evidence documenting his disability. The Court concluded that, since the issue to be decided was the beneficiary's medical condition, written evidence would be highly probative and the oral hearing requested by the plaintiff would not have led to more accurate decision making.

5. *Mathews* Creates a Flexible Test

In sum, while *Mathews* provides the rule for determining the amount of process due, the factors are sufficiently vague that courts retain a great deal of leeway to judge cases according to their own sense of efficiency and equity.

6. Due Process Also Requires an Impartial Decision Maker

Beyond *Mathews*, due process requires an impartial decision maker. Usually impartiality is decided based on the particular facts of the situation.

7. Pecuniary Interests Constitute a *Per Se* Due Process Violation

One situation where impartiality is *per se* questioned is when the decision maker has a pecuniary interest in the outcome of the issue.

8. Personal Animus Is Also a *Per Se* Due Process Violation

Due process is also violated where the decision maker has a personal animus against the party.

9. Prejudgment of Adjudicative Facts Is Also Often a Due Process Violation

Prejudgment of an issue can be a problem if it is thought that the adjudicator has prejudged adjudicative facts about the party's claim; however, prejudgment about the law or more legislative-type facts is generally considered less of a problem.

H. FORMAL ADJUDICATION

1. The APA Calls for Trial–Type Procedures in Formal Adjudication

The APA has detailed procedures for formal adjudicative processes. In general, these procedures, set forth at 5 U.S.C. §§ 554, 556 and 557, provide for the types of procedures normally found in trial courts.

2. Trial–Type Procedures Call for Oral Hearings, Cross–Examination and Decisions on the Record

Thus, parties have the right to request an oral hearing, to call witnesses and cross-examine the other side's witnesses, and to have a decision made on the record.

3. The ALJ Can Either Make the Decision or Recommend the Decision to Be Made by the Agency Head

The APA authorizes administrative law judges (ALJs) to reach a decision for the agency, or simply to recommend a decision to the agency head, who then makes the decision. Even if the ALJ makes the actual decision, agencies may if they wish provide for an appeal procedure to the agency head.

4. The APA Restricts *Ex Parte* Communications With Agency Personnel

Ex parte communications between administrative judges (ALJs) and others are the subject of two separate APA provisions. Section 554(d) of the APA provides explicit rules governing the *ex parte* communications of ALJs and agency heads conducting formal adjudications.

5. The Internal *Ex Parte* Communication Ban Applies to ALJs

That provision prohibits ALJs from speaking to any person about a fact in issue in the case, except on notice and opportunity to participate to the other side, and prohibits ALJS from being supervised by agency employees performing investigative or prosecutorial functions.

6. Agency Heads May Speak With Agency Personnel

Agency heads, who sometimes hear cases on appeal from ALJs, are exempt from these rules; however, witnesses and prosecutors are still limited to participating only in their respective capacities.

7. The APA Also Restricts *Ex Parte* Communications With Private Parties

Section 557(d) deals with *ex parte* communications between agency adjudicators (ALJs or agency heads) and persons outside the agency. It prohibits any such communication "relative to the merits of the proceeding."

8. The External *Ex Parte* Communications Ban Extends to the Adjudicator and to the Private Party

Note that the prohibition extends to communications initiated by both the adjudicator and the private party.

9. If *Ex Parte* Communications With a Private Party Occur the Adjudicator Must Memorialize and Disclose Them

If such a communication does occur, the adjudicator must describe its substance in a memorandum that is placed in the adjudicatory record, and provide an opportunity for parties to respond.

10. Knowing *Ex Parte* Communications Can Lead to a Ruling Against the Violating Party

If such a communication is knowingly made by a party—that is, made with knowledge that it is an *ex parte* communication—the adjudicator has the authority, but is not required, to punish it by ruling against that party on the merits.

■ CHAPTER THREE: CHOICE OF PROCEDURES AND NON–LEGISLATIVE RULES

A. NON–LEGISLATIVE RULES DEFINED

The term "non-legislative rule" extends to a variety of administrative pronouncements such as adjudicative rules, policy statements and interpretive rules. Even though such rules are not necessarily binding, they constitute "rules" because they fit the APA's definition of a "rule"—"the whole or a part of an agency statement of general or particular applicability and future effect designed to implement, interpret, or prescribe law or policy. . . . " 5 U.S.C.A. § 551(4).

B. DISTINGUISHED FROM LEGISLATIVE RULES

Non-legislative rules can be distinguished from "legislative rules" by virtue of the way they are created. Legislative rules are promulgated using the APA's rulemaking procedures, and are legally binding. 5 U.S.C.A. § 553. As we shall see, "non-legislative rules" can be created using a variety of procedures.

C. TYPES OF NON–LEGISLATIVE RULES

Under Section 553 of the Administrative Procedure Act, there are two different types of non-legislative rules: "interpretative rules" and "general statements of policy." Both are exempt from APA Section 553's notice and comment procedures. However, "adjudicative rules," "rules" announced by agencies in adjudicative proceedings, also qualify as non-legislative rules.

1. Preference for Legislative Rules

In general, legislative procedures are considered to be a fairer, and more appropriate, method for making rules. There are two reasons. First, since legislative rules generally have prospective effect, whereas adjudicative rules are frequently applied retroactively, legislative rules provide regulated entities with greater notice regarding regulatory requirements and an opportunity to bring their conduct into compliance. Second, since legislative procedures are subject to rulemaking processes (meaning that the agency must announce the proposed rule and give interested parties the opportunity to comment and provide input), they ensure greater public participation and input into the rulemaking process.

2. Choice of Adjudication Over Rulemaking

In *Securities and Exchange Commission v. Chenery Corporation*, 332 U.S. 194, 67 S.Ct. 1575, 91 L.Ed. 1995 (1947), even though the United States Supreme

Court expressed a preference for legislative procedures over adjudicative procedures, the Court held that administrative agencies have discretion about whether to articulate new rules legislatively or adjudicatively. In other words, they can articulate new "rules" and "policies" in adjudicative proceedings.

3. Need for Adjudicative Rules

Chenery II went on to note that "[not] every principle essential to the effective administration of a statute can or should be cast immediately into the mold of a general rule. Some principles must await their own development, while others must be adjusted to meet particular, unforeseeable situations. In performing its important functions in these respects, therefore, an administrative agency must be equipped to act either by general rule or by individual order. To insist upon one form of action to the exclusion of the other is to exalt form over necessity."

4. Impossibility of Creating All Rules Legislatively

In *Chenery II*, the Court went on to suggest that it would be difficult for administrative agencies to articulate all policies legislatively.

5. Adjudicative Rules May Be Valid Even if Retroactively Applied

Chenery II also recognized that adjudicative rules may cause unfairness if they are retroactively applied, but the Court held that the mere presence of retroactivity is "not necessarily fatal to its validity."

6. *Chenery II* Affirmed

Chenery II's holding has been reaffirmed in later cases, including *National Labor Relations Board v. Bell Aerospace Company Division of Textron, Inc.*, 416 U.S. 267, 94 S.Ct. 1757, 40 L.Ed.2d 134 (1974), and *NLRB v. Wyman–Gordon Co.*, 394 U.S. 759, 89 S.Ct. 1426, 22 L.Ed.2d 709 (1969).

7. Agency Preference for Adjudicative Procedures

Many administrative agencies prefer to use adjudicative processes to create rules because those processes are not as public. In addition, adjudicative processes are frequently easier and less expensive than national rulemaking proceedings. Finally, adjudicative processes are not subject to many of the procedural requirements applicable to legislative proceedings (e.g., cost-benefit analyses, OMB review, and congressional reviews).

8. Wyman–Gordon and the Excelsior Rule

In *National Labor Relations Board v. Wyman–Gordon Co.*, 394 U.S. 759, 89 S.Ct. 1426, 22 L.Ed.2d 709 (1969), the United States Supreme Court dealt with the so-called *Excelsior Underwear* rule. That rule was articulated in an NLRB case, *Excelsior Underwear*, and involved an attempt by the NLRB to create an adjudicative rule using quasi-legislative procedures. Although the "rule" was created in an adjudicative proceeding, the NLRB contacted certain interested parties and invited them to submit comments on the proposed rule. The NLRB suggested that its new "rule" would be applied only prospectively.

a. Judicial Criticism of the *Excelsior Underwear* Procedure

In *Wyman–Gordon*, the Court criticized the NLRB's approach, and suggested that legislative procedures constitute a preferable method for articulating new rules.

b. *Excelsior Underwear* Did Not Create a Valid Legislative Rule

In addition, the Court held that the *Excelsior Underwear* rule did not create a valid legislative rule. There had been no compliance with legislative procedures since a NOPR had not been published in the *Federal Register* and the NLRB had not invited all interested parties to submit comments.

c. *Excelsior Underwear* Did Not Create a Valid Adjudicative Rule

In addition, the Court concluded that the NLRB had not created a valid adjudicative rule since the rule was not applied in the *Excelsior Underwear* case. As a result, the rule was simply dicta.

d. Wyman–Gordon Was Forced to Comply With the Gist of the *Excelsior Underwear* Rule

Nonetheless, the Court ordered Wyman–Gordon to comply because the rule was validly imposed in the *Wyman–Gordon* case itself, and the rule constituted a valid adjudicative rule in that context.

D. OTHER NON–LEGISLATIVE RULES (POLICY STATEMENTS AND INTERPRETIVE STATEMENTS)

Section 553 of the APA recognizes two types of non-legislative rules: interpretive rules and statements of policy. An *interpretive rule* is a statement "issued by an agency to advise the public of the agency's construction of the statutes and rules which it administers." Attorney General's Manual on the Administrative Procedure Act 30 n. 3 (1947). A *policy statement* is a statement "issued by an agency to advise the public prospectively of the manner in which the agency proposes to exercise a discretionary power." *Id*. The distinction between these two types of non-legislative rules will be considered in greater detail below. For now, it is sufficient to know that these rules warn the public of an agency's interpretation of a statute or regulation, or reflect the agency's views on policy issues.

1. Justifications for Using Non–Legislative Rules

Just as adjudicative rules have a place in the administrative system, other non-legislative rules have a place as well. Non-legislative rules serve a valid informational function by advising regulated entities about the agency's views regarding the meaning of a statute or regulation, and the agency's enforcement policy. In addition, non-legislative rules provide guidance to agency personnel who must interpret and apply the provisions.

2. Concerns Regarding Non–Legislative Rules

Even if a regulated entity believes that an agency's interpretation of a statute or regulation is incorrect or unfair, the regulated entity may feel pressure to comply with the agency's interpretation. Otherwise, it risks the possibility of an enforcement action with possible fines and penalties. Of course, the regulated entity can challenge the agency's interpretation, but such challenges can be time-consuming and expensive.

3. Publication Requirements

Even though the APA exempts policy statements from rulemaking procedures, it does require agencies to publish in the *Federal Register* "statements of general policy or interpretations of general applicability formulated and adopted by the agency." *Id*. § 552(a)(1)(D). However, courts rarely sanction agencies for failure to publish their interpretations and policy statements. *See* James T. O'Reilly, Federal Information Disclosure, § 6.05 at 6–19 (2d ed. 1995).

4. Disguised Legislative Rules

Some regulated entities challenge policy statements on the basis that they are really legislative rules and therefore should be subject to rulemaking procedures. Some courts agree, holding that some policy statements constitute legislative rules when they impose a new "duty" with "binding effect."

5. Difficulty of Characterization

Even though an interpretive rule or policy statement does not literally impose new "duties" or "rights and obligations," it is important to realize that many interpretive rules and policy statements can be treated like rules imposing new "rights" and "duties." As previously noted, regulated entities are reluctant to ignore agency statements of interpretations or policy for fear of prosecution.

E. DEFERENCE TO ADJUDICATIVE AND NON–LEGISLATIVE RULES

Moreover, even though the courts have the authority to independently interpret statutory and regulatory provisions, courts frequently defer to agency interpretations of those provisions. Courts often defer even though an agency has stated its interpretation in the form of an adjudicative rule or non-legislative rule.

1. Scope of Deference

There has been some disagreement about what standard of deference should apply to agency interpretations, especially to non-legislative rules such as policy statements and administrative interpretations.

a. *Skidmore* Deference

In some instances, courts apply so-called *Skidmore* deference in which they are not compelled to accept administrative interpretations, but instead treat them as a "a body of experience and informed judgment to which courts and litigants may properly resort for guidance." *Skidmore v. Swift & Co.*, 323 U.S. 134, 65 S.Ct. 161, 89 L.Ed. 124 (1944).

b. *Chevron* Deference

Instead of *Skidmore* deference, courts sometimes apply an alternate deference standard referred to as *Chevron* deference. Under *Chevron* deference, if Congress' intent regarding the meaning of a provision is unclear, the courts should accept an agency's "reasonable" interpretation of that provision. *Chevron, U.S.A., Inc. v. Natural Resources Defense Council, Inc.*, 467 U.S. 837, 104 S.Ct. 2778, 81 L.Ed.2d 694 (1984).

c. Distinguishing *Chevron* Deference and *Skidmore* Deference

As the language suggests, *Chevron* is potentially more deferential to administrative action than *Skidmore*. Instead of requiring a reviewing court to independently determine the meaning of a regulatory provision, giving an agency interpretation the weight it is due after consideration of a variety of factors, *Chevron* requires a reviewing court to accept a "reasonable" interpretation of an ambiguous regulatory provision.

2. Application to Non–Legislative Rules

The Court has vacillated regarding whether *Chevron* deference or *Skidmore* deference should be applied to non-legislative rules. *Chevron* itself involved application of the *Chevron* standard to a legislative rule.

a. The *Christensen* Decision

The Court has applied *Skidmore* deference to some non-legislative rules. For example, in *Christensen v. Harris County*, 529 U.S. 576, 120 S.Ct. 1655, 146 L.Ed.2d 621 (2000), the Court applied *Skidmore* to an agency's "opinion letter" construing the meaning of a federal statute.

b. The *Mead* Decision

In *United States v. Mead Corporation*, 533 U.S. 218, 121 S.Ct. 2164, 150 L.Ed.2d 292 (2001), the Court refused to apply *Chevron* deference to a "ruling letter." However, *Mead* suggested that the Court had applied *Chevron* deference to some interpretations articulated by less formal means than rulemaking.

c. The *Barnhart* Decision

The Court further muddied the waters in its later decision in *Barnhart v. Walton*, 535 U.S. 212, 122 S.Ct. 1265, 152 L.Ed.2d 330 (2002). In that case, although the agency had articulated its interpretation in a legislative rule, the rule was of relatively recent duration and it was argued that it did not deserve deference because it was developed in response to the litigation. The Court concluded that *Chevron* deference should apply anyway because the interpretation was of long standing, albeit articulated in less formal ways.

3. Deference to An Agency's Interpretation of Its Own Regulations

In general, the Court has been strongly inclined to defer to an agency's interpretation of its own regulations.

a. The Holding in *Bowles v. Seminole Rock*

In its landmark decision, *Bowles v. Seminole Rock & Sand Co.*, 325 U.S. 410, 65 S.Ct. 1215, 89 L.Ed. 1700 (1945), the Court concluded that: "The intention of Congress or the principles of the Constitution in some situations may be relevant in the first instance in choosing between various constructions. But the ultimate criterion is the administrative interpretation, which becomes of controlling weight unless it is plainly erroneous or inconsistent with the regulation."

b. **The Justifications for Deferring to an Agency's Interpretation of Its Own Regulation**

Courts are more inclined to defer to an agency's interpretation of its own regulation because the agency was the promulgator of the regulation and therefore is more likely to be cognizant of the regulation's intended meaning and scope, as well as of the agency's own original intent. In addition, the agency is acting in a sphere of delegated authority.

F. RETROACTIVITY

In general, retroactivity is disfavored in the law. As a simple matter of fairness, if not due process, regulated entities are entitled to fair notice of the standards with which they must comply, and an opportunity to bring their conduct into compliance with those standards. Because retroactively applied rules are announced after the fact, they have the potential to deprive regulated entities of fair notice.

1. Retroactive Regulations

Although most administrative regulations are issued with prospective effect, it is sometimes permissible for agencies to promulgate regulations with retroactive effect. In *Bowen v. Georgetown University Hospital*, 488 U.S. 204, 109 S.Ct. 468, 102 L.Ed.2d 493 (1988), the Court held that an agency may not give a regulation retroactive effect absent explicit congressional authorization.

2. Retroactive Interpretations

When an agency adopts a rule with prospective effect, retroactivity problems may still arise as the rule is interpreted and applied.

a. **Vagueness and Ambiguity**

It is not uncommon for regulatory provisions to suffer from vagueness or ambiguity. Indeed, the concept of deference itself, including *Chevron* deference, is premised on uncertainty regarding the meaning of regulatory provisions.

b. **Retroactive Application of Agency Pronouncements**

If a regulatory provision suffers from vagueness or ambiguity, that provision will ultimately need interpretation in the context of a regula tory adjudication or an agency-issued interpretation. In some instances, these interpretations are applied retroactively. Interpretations announced in adjudications are usually applied retroactively.

3. Interpretations and the Right to Notice

In *General Electric Company v. U.S. Environmental Protection Agency*, 53 F.3d 1324 (D.C.Cir.1995), although the Court accepted an agency's interpretation of its own regulation, the court refused to allow the agency to apply the interpretation retroactively.

4. Methods of Giving Notice

However, as *General Electric* also recognized, "in many cases the agency's pre-enforcement efforts to bring about compliance will provide adequate notice. As a result, even if an interpretation is retroactively applied, the regulated entity may not be able to claim lack of notice."

a. Direct Notice

Sometimes, agencies provide direct notice to regulated entities. If, for example, an agency informs a regulated party that it must seek a permit for a particular action, but the party begins acting without seeking a permit, the agency's pre-violation contact with the regulated party might be regarded as adequate notice. As a result, the court might be more inclined to impose liability for noncompliance if the agency's interpretation was permissible.

b. Indirect Notice

As *General Electric* held, even when the agency has not provided a regulated entity with direct notice of its interpretation, the regulated entity may be on constructive notice: "If, by reviewing the regulations and other public statements issued by the agency, a regulated party acting in good faith would be able to identify, with 'ascertainable certainty,' the standards with which the agency expects parties to conform, then the agency has fairly notified a petitioner of the agency's interpretation."

G. ESTOPPEL

For decades, the accepted wisdom was that the government may not be "estopped" in the same sense in which a private individual might be estopped.

For example, in *Federal Crop Ins. Corporation v. Merrill*, 332 U.S. 380, 68 S.Ct. 1, 92 L.Ed. 10 (1947), the Court applied estoppel when a government agent promised a farmer that government insurance covered his crops. Because the program did not cover individuals in the farmer's situation, the Court held that the farmer could not recover notwithstanding the agency's prior representations to the contrary. The Court expressed concern that federal law precluded recovery in that case, and that an agent's misstatement could not overcome the requirements of federal law.

1. Justifications for the General Rule

The prohibition against estopping the government reflects a judicial intent to protect the public purse. In many cases, either Congress or administrative regulations provide guidelines regarding the expenditure of public funds. As a result, if Congress has provided for money to be spent in a particular way, or under defined criteria, courts are reluctant to require agencies to spend money inconsistently with the law or the criteria based solely on the representations of subordinate governmental officials.

2. The *Richmond* Exception

In *Office Of Personnel Management v. Richmond*, 496 U.S. 414, 110 S.Ct. 2465, 110 L.Ed.2d 387 (1990), the Court qualified *Merrill* by noting that "erroneous oral and written advice given by a Government employee to a benefits claimant may give rise to estoppel against the Government and so entitle the claimant to a monetary payment not otherwise permitted by law." However, relying on the Appropriations Clause of the Constitution, Art. I, § 9, cl. 7, the Court concluded that an estoppel claim could not force the government to pay out money prohibited by law.

3. Other Exceptions

In *United States v. Pennsylvania Industrial Chemical Corporation*, 411 U.S. 655, 93 S.Ct. 1804, 36 L.Ed.2d 567 (1973), the Court held that an individual, who had reasonably relied on statements made by a government agent, could not be criminally prosecuted when he acted consistently with that advice. Criminal sanctions are regarded as particularly onerous and fair notice is a prerequisite.

4. Inconsistent Application

Even though estoppel principles might not explicitly apply to the government, courts might apply a form of estoppel when an agency has taken inconsistent positions regarding the meaning of a statutory or regulatory provision. Courts have held that agency action is arbitrary and capricious if the agency acts inconsistently with past decisions without explaining the basis for the change. Also, to the extent that the agency is asking a court to defer to its new interpretation, courts may refuse deference because the agency has not been consistent. In *North Haven Board of Education v. Bell*, 456 U.S. 512, 102 S.Ct. 1912, 72 L.Ed.2d 299 (1982), for example, the Supreme Court rejected an administrative interpretation because the agency had changed its interpretation of a regulation several times, once during the course of the judicial proceedings. The Court concluded that there was no interpretation to which to defer.

5. More on Inconsistency

But the prohibition against inconsistent application is not absolute. In *Rust v. Sullivan*, 500 U.S. 173, 111 S.Ct. 1759, 114 L.Ed.2d 233 (1991), the Court held that consistency is not necessary to obtain deference, at least where the agency justifies the change with a reasoned analysis.

■ CHAPTER FOUR: THE AVAILABILITY OF JUDICIAL REVIEW

A. SEVERAL PREREQUISITES MUST BE MET BEFORE A PARTY CAN OBTAIN JUDICIAL REVIEW

A number of prerequisites must be satisfied before a party seeking judicial review of agency action can have its case heard by a court. This chapter sets forth the most important of these prerequisites.

B. JURISDICTION DOES NOT PRESENT SERIOUS PROBLEMS TODAY

An essential part of obtaining judicial review is that the reviewing court have jurisdiction over the case. Many statutes authorizing administrative action explicitly confer jurisdiction on a federal court (usually although not always an appellate court) to hear challenges to that action. If not, a general jurisdictional grant, such as the general federal question jurisdiction statute, will suffice. The APA does not grant jurisdiction.

C. AGENCY ACTION MUST BE REVIEWABLE BY COURTS

Judicial action must also be reviewable by courts. Courts have interpreted the APA as enacting a broad presumption in favor of judicial review. 5 U.S.C. § 701 provides for judicial review of agency action except "to the extent that (1) statutes preclude judicial review; or (2) agency action is committed to agency discretion by law." Both of these exceptions are narrow. First, courts give narrow readings to statutes precluding judicial review, and require that Congress be explicit in its desire to preclude review. Second, the "committed to agency discretion by law" exception is construed narrowly, to apply only in situations where the law is written so broadly that there is no law to apply. However, agency decisions whether or not to prosecute alleged statutory or regulatory violations are presumptively unreviewable.

D. STANDING REQUIRES A PROPER PLAINTIFF

Standing—the doctrine that examines whether the correct plaintiff is suing—has roots both in Article III of the Constitution's requirement that there be a "case or controversy," and in prudential concerns about the appropriateness of that party as a plaintiff.

1. Article III Requires Injury, Causation and Redressability

Article III of the Constitution limits federal courts' jurisdiction to "cases and controversies." The Supreme Court reads this requirement as imposing a three-part requirement for standing. In order for a plaintiff to have Article III standing, the plaintiff (1) must be injured, in a way (2) caused by the defendant, and (3) redressable by the court.

2. Many Types of Injuries Satisfy the Article III Requirement

A broad array of types of injury satisfy this requirement. For example, injury includes not only an impairment of a common-law-protected interest, such as physical integrity, contractual rights or property, but also impairment of scenic or aesthetic interests. Moreover, Congress by statute may create rights, the deprivation of which constitutes injury for Article III standing purposes. However, injury must have occurred, or must be imminent.

3. Causation and Redressability

Moreover, Congress by statute may create rights, the deprivation of which constitutes injury for Article III standing purposes. These concepts have special roles in administrative law, making it harder for plaintiffs to satisfy causation and redressability when challenging agency action that takes the form of incentives to private parties to act in desired ways.

4. Prudential Standing Limits Exist But Can Be Waived

Standing also implicates prudential concerns. Because these limitations are not based in the Constitution but rather on prudential concerns, courts and Congress can override them.

5. The APA Sets the Limit for Prudential Standing in Administrative Law Cases

In § 702 of the APA Congress set forth the prudential standing limit. Section 702 states that a person "suffering legal wrong because of agency action, or adversely affected or aggrieved by agency action within the meaning of the relevant statute" may sue. The Court has interpreted this language to require that the plaintiff be "arguably within the zone of interests" sought to be protected by the statute. The "zone of interests" test is easy for plaintiffs to satisfy.

E. THE LAWSUIT MUST BE PROPERLY TIMED

1. Courts Try to Avoid Premature Review of Agency Action

Judicial review must be appropriately timed. In general, courts attempt to avoid reviewing agency action before that action is final and before the agency has completed its work. Courts apply this principle through the doctrines of exhaustion, ripeness, and finality. The "primary jurisdiction" doctrine also plays this role, indirectly.

2. Exhaustion

The exhaustion doctrine is highly discretionary, except when Congress specifies a particular rule to be followed. In cases governed by the APA, § 704 excuses a person from having to exhaust internal agency appeals procedures unless the agency by rule provides that during the pendency of those procedures the initial decision will be inoperative.

3. Agency Action Must Be Ripe

In *Abbott Labs v. Gardner*, 387 U.S. 136, 87 S.Ct. 1507, 18 L.Ed.2d 681 (1967), the Supreme Court held that ripeness requires evaluation of whether (1) the agency action is fit for judicial review at the current time and (2) the extent to which deferring judicial review would cause significant hardship to the parties. The first prong of this test is generally understood to rest, at least in part, on Article III concerns, while the second prong concerns itself with the prudential idea that judicial review is more appropriately delayed when there is little risk that the delay will harm any party. Subject to Article III concerns, Congress can also either mandate or prohibit early, or "pre-enforcement" review of agency action—that is, review before an agency actually brings an enforcement action against a party.

4. An Agency Action Must Be Final Before a Court Will Review It

Finally, agency action must be final before it can be challenged in court, unless Congress dispenses with this requirement. The Supreme Court has established a two-part test for determining finality. "First, the action must mark the 'consummation' of the agency's decision-making process—it must not be of a merely tentative or interlocutory nature. And second, the action must be one by which 'rights or obligations have been determined,' or from which 'legal consequences will follow.'" *Bennett v. Spear*, 520 U.S. 154, 177–178, 117 S.Ct. 1154, 137 L.Ed.2d 281 (1997).

5. The Doctrine of Primary Jurisdiction Sometimes Delays Judicial Resolution of Suits Between Private Parties

The doctrine of primary jurisdiction arises when two private parties litigate an issue in court that should be passed on first by an administrative agency, in the interest of effective and uniform national regulation. In such a case, the doctrine allows a court to stay its proceedings in order for the relevant agency to examine the facts and make a determination.

■ CHAPTER FIVE: INSPECTIONS, REPORTS & SUBPOENAS

A. INTRODUCTION

Administrative agencies thrive on information. They use information to set policy through the promulgation of rules and regulations, to keep Congress advised regarding various matters, and to enforce regulatory requirements and prosecute companies for civil and criminal violations. Agencies obtain this information in different ways: they conduct inspections and searches; they require persons to submit information or produce documents to the agency; and they require persons to keep records which the government is allowed to inspect. This chapter considers the legal and constitutional authority of agencies to acquire information.

B. INSPECTIONS

A number of agencies regularly inspect buildings and work sites. Health inspectors enter restaurants to determine whether food preparation and service areas are clean, as well as to see whether food is being kept under healthy conditions. Inspectors from the Occupational Safety and Health Administration (OSHA) examine construction and factory sites to make sure that workers are employed in safe and healthy conditions. In some instances, administrative officials even seek to enter people's homes or yards. Child welfare officials, for example, enter homes looking for abused or neglected children.

1. Legal Authority to Inspect

An agency's authority to inspect is defined by its enabling act. If Congress (or a state legislature) has not authorized an agency to conduct administrative inspections, it has no legal authority to do so. Moreover, an agency's authority to inspect is co-extensive with its statutory authorization.

2. Fourth Amendment Limitations

As we shall see, agency authority to inspect is also limited by the Fourth Amendment. Through the Fourteenth Amendment, state agencies are also subject to the Fourth Amendment.

a. Prior Precedent Regarding the Fourth Amendment

Until the 1960s, there was doubt about whether the Fourth Amendment required a warrant for administrative inspections. For example, in *Frank v. Maryland*, 359 U.S. 360, 79 S.Ct. 804, 3 L.Ed.2d 877 (1959), the Supreme Court held that the warrant requirement did not apply to administrative inspections because they "touch at most upon the periphery of the important interests safeguarded by the Fourteenth Amendment's protection against official intrusion."

b. Camara v. Municipal Court

However, in *Camara v. Municipal Court*, 387 U.S. 523, 87 S.Ct. 1727, 18 L.Ed.2d 930 (1967), the Court overruled *Frank* and held that the Fourth Amendment applies to administrative inspections.

c. Warrant Requirement

Camara also made clear that, in the administrative context, the Fourth Amendment requires the government to obtain a warrant based on "probable cause." Absent a warrant, or the consent of the property owner (or some other exception to the warrant requirement), a search is deemed to be "unreasonable" and therefore invalid under the Fourth Amendment.

d. The Requirement of Probable Cause

Camara also held that a warrant must be based on "probable cause." However, the Court held that the warrant requirement would not be specifically applied in the administrative context and might be satisfied by so-called "area inspections" even though "such inspections are 'unavoidably based on its [the agency's] appraisal of conditions in the area as a whole, not on its knowledge of conditions in each particular building.' "

e. Support for Area Inspections

Camara further justified "area inspections."

f. "Reasonable" Legislative or Administrative Standards

In other contexts, the Court has focused on whether the agency has established "reasonable legislative or administrative standards" for conducting inspections under the regulatory scheme.

g. Permissible Grounds for Warrantless Inspections

Despite the Court's preference for a warrant, the Court indicated that warrantless inspections have traditionally been upheld in a variety of contexts including "emergency situations. *See North American Cold Storage Co. v. City of Chicago*, 211 U.S. 306, 29 S.Ct. 101, 53 L.Ed. 195 (1908) (seizure of unwholesome food); *Jacobson v. Commonwealth of Massachusetts*, 197 U.S. 11, 25 S.Ct. 358, 49 L.Ed. 643 (1905) (compulsory smallpox vaccination); *Compagnie Francaise De Navigation a Vapeur v. Louisiana State Board of Health*, 186 U.S. 380, 22 S.Ct. 811, 46 L.Ed. 1209 (1902) (health quarantine); *Kroplin v. Truax*, 119 Ohio St. 610, 165 N.E. 498 (1929) (summary destruction of tubercular cattle)." However, the Court noted that routine area inspections do not present emergency or exigent circumstances.

h. *Camara's* Extension to Businesses

In *See v. City of Seattle*, 387 U.S. 541, 87 S.Ct. 1737, 18 L.Ed.2d 943 (1967), *Camara's* holding was extended to inspections of commercial properties.

The Court held that a "businessman, like the occupant of a residence, has a constitutional right to go about his business free from unreasonable official entries upon his private property." In later cases, the warrant requirement has been extended to a variety of other administrative inspections.

i. Closely Regulated Businesses

Following *Camara*, the Court recognized an exception from the warrant requirement for businesses and industries that had long been subject to close government regulation. The theory was that a person entering such a business had a reduced expectation of privacy. *See Colonnade Catering Corp. v. United States*, 397 U.S. 72, 90 S.Ct. 774, 25 L.Ed.2d 60 (1970) (liquor dealers); *United States v. Biswell*, 406 U.S. 311, 92 S.Ct. 1593, 32 L.Ed.2d 87 (1972) (firearms dealers); *Donovan v. Dewey*, 452 U.S. 594, 101 S.Ct. 2534, 69 L.Ed.2d 262 (1981) (underground mines); *New York v. Burger*, 482 U.S. 691, 107 S.Ct. 2636, 96 L.Ed.2d 601 (1987) (auto junkyard). In regard to such businesses, the Court asked first whether the searches serve an important government purpose and are necessary to achieve that purpose. The Court also inquired whether the statute authorizing the searches provides protections substituting for a warrant— providing notice of searches to the owner, limiting the scope of the search, and limiting the discretion of the inspecting officer.

j. OSHA Inspections

In *Marshall v. Barlow's, Inc.*, 436 U.S. 307, 98 S.Ct. 1816, 56 L.Ed.2d 305 (1978), the Court refused to extend the "closely regulated business" exception to businesses subject to the Occupational Safety and Health Act. The Court concluded that application of the exception to OSHA inspections would create a gaping hole in Fourth Amendment protections since virtually every industry in the United States is subject to OSHA. In addition, the Court doubted that the warrant requirement would "impose serious burdens on the inspection system or the courts, [would] prevent inspections necessary to enforce the statute, or [would] make them less effective. In the first place, the great majority of businessmen can be expected in the normal course to consent to inspection without warrant."

k. Administrative Inspections and Consent

Even though *Camara* imposes a warrant requirement, the reality is that most administrative inspections are conducted without a warrant by the consent of the parties. Most businesses recognize that there is little to be gained by refusing consent in the ordinary situation. If consent is refused, the inspector will most likely return with a warrant, but may not be in the best of humor and may be more likely to find violations. For these reasons, many industry groups advise their members to willingly consent to administrative inspections.

l. The *Burger* Exception

In *New York v. Burger*, 482 U.S. 691, 107 S.Ct. 2636, 96 L.Ed.2d 601 (1987), the Court extended the "closely regulated industry" exception to what seemed like traditional criminal conduct. That case involved the New York Vehicle and Traffic Law which provided that persons engaged in the business of vehicle dismantling were required to have a license and to keep records of the vehicles coming into their possession. The Court rejected Burger's claim that the search was unconstitutional, concluding that there was no constitutional significance to the fact that police undertook the inspections or that they might find evidence of crime in addition to evidence of regulatory violations (such as failure to have a license or keep appropriate records).

3. Remedies for Illegal Inspections

Even though *Camara* loosened the probable cause requirements for administrative searches, illegal inspections do occur. Sometimes, an agency obtains a warrant but the warrant is invalidly issued. In other cases, as in *Barlow's*, the agency searches without a warrant when one is required. In addition, the police may conduct an illegal search and give the results to administrative officials. In these contexts, remedial questions arise.

a. Monetary Remedies

When governmental officials illegally enter a home or business, they may be subjected to various remedies. For example, they be liable in tort under state law (*e.g.*, trespass) or held liable under federal law. When federal, state, or local officials violate a citizen's Fourth Amendment right to be free from unreasonable searches and seizures, they can also be sued under the Constitution itself, *Bivens v. Six Unknown Named Agents of the Federal Bureau of Narcotics*, 403 U.S. 388, 91 S.Ct. 1999, 29 L.Ed.2d 619 (1971), or under 42 U.S.C.A. § 1983 (authorizing suits against state officials who infringe citizens' "rights, privileges, or immunities secured by the Constitution and laws" of the United States).

b.   The Exclusionary Evidence Rule

Another potential remedy is the exclusionary evidence rule. The federal courts have long prohibited federal prosecutors from using evidence seized in violation of a defendant's constitutional rights in criminal cases. *Weeks v. United States*, 232 U.S. 383, 34 S.Ct. 341, 58 L.Ed. 652 (1914). In *Mapp v. Ohio*, 367 U.S. 643, 81 S.Ct. 1684, 6 L.Ed.2d 1081 (1961), the Court extended this rule to state prosecutions. However, neither decision applied the exclusionary rule to deny administrative agencies the use of information in administrative cases.

(1)   United States v. Janis

In *United States v. Janis*, 428 U.S. 433, 96 S.Ct. 3021, 49 L.Ed.2d 1046 (1976), the Court refused to apply the exclusionary rule in an administrative proceeding when evidence was seized in good faith by criminal law enforcement officials who were found to have acted unconstitutionally.

(2)   Intra–Agency Exclusion and Deterrence

Although *Janis* refused to apply the exclusionary rule in a civil context, the decision did not rule out the possibility that the rule might be applied in some civil proceedings when the deterrent effect of exclusion might be served. One of the motivating factors behind the *Janis* decision was the idea that the evidence had been seized by the police for use in criminal proceedings. The Court concluded that the police are motivated to obtain illegal evidence for use in criminal proceedings, but are not motivated by the possibility of using the evidence in civil proceedings. As a result, *Janis* left open the possibility that the exclusionary rule might be applied when administrative officials seize evidence for use in civil proceedings. In that intra-agency use of illegal evidence, application of the exclusionary rule might deter future governmental misconduct.

(3)   INS v. Lopez–Mendoza

However, in *INS v. Lopez–Mendoza*, 468 U.S. 1032, 104 S.Ct. 3479, 82 L.Ed.2d 778 (1984), the Court refused to apply the exclusionary evidence rule in an intra-agency context. In *Lopez–Mendoza*, a suspect admitted that he was an illegal alien during an illegal arrest. When the Immigration and Naturalization Service (INS) sought to use the admission in a deportation proceeding, the suspect moved to exclude the evidence. Nevertheless, the Court concluded that the "likely deterrent value of the exclusionary rule in a civil deportation proceeding" was limited.

C. "SPECIAL NEEDS" SEARCHES

Many administrative agencies also conduct so-called "special needs" searches and the Court has dispensed with both the warrant requirement and the probable cause requirement in this context. Illustrative are the imposition of mandatory drug tests for employees and students. As is the case with inspections, the question arises whether drug tests can be required absent a particularized showing of probable cause that would justify a warrant. Many of these searches have been upheld.

1. "Need" Versus "Intrusion" Test

In the special needs context, the Court has continued to focus on the Fourth Amendment requirement of reasonableness. However, in deciding whether it is "reasonable" for an agency to proceed without a warrant and whether it can also dispense with the requirement of probable cause, the Court balances the "need" for the search against the level of "intrusion" caused thereby.

2. The *Skinner* Decision

In *Skinner v. Railway Labor Executives' Association*, 489 U.S. 602, 109 S.Ct. 1402, 103 L.Ed.2d 639 (1989), the Court upheld Federal Railroad Administration (FRA) regulations mandating blood and urine testing of railroad employees involved in "major" train accidents, and authorizing railroads to administer breath and urine tests to employees who violate certain safety rules.

3. *Earls* and Drug Testing of Students

In *Board of Education of Independent School District No. 92 of Pottawatomie County v. Earls*, 536 U.S. 822, 122 S.Ct. 2559, 153 L.Ed.2d 735 (2002), the Court extended the special needs exception to a high school program involving suspicionless, warrantless, drug testing of students involved in extra-curricular activities.

4. *Ferguson* & Drug Testing for Pregnant Women

In *Ferguson v. City of Charleston*, 532 U.S. 67, 121 S.Ct. 1281, 149 L.Ed.2d 205 (2001), a city instituted a program whereby the local hospital, without the knowledge or consent of the patients, would perform drug screens on the urine samples provided by pregnant patients and, if the drug test was positive, the hospital would provide the results to local law enforcement. The Court found that the program violated the Fourth Amendment.

D. RECORDKEEPING AND REPORTING REQUIREMENTS

Agencies also require individuals and corporations to keep and report information for a variety of purposes and in a variety of manners.

1. Collection of Statistical Data

Some agencies gather statistics. For example, the United States Department of Commerce's Bureau of the Census conducts a decennial census mandated by the Constitution, and also conducts more targeted data collections as required by Congress (e.g., to monitor the economy). The United States Department of Energy's Energy Information Administration collects data regarding oil imports into the United States.

2. Regulatory Monitoring

Agencies also gather information designed to monitor compliance with their regulatory programs. For instance, under the Clean Water Act, those who hold permits to discharge pollutants must submit monitoring reports. Agencies also gather information to help them determine whether statutes or regulations have been violated, or to gather evidence to proceed against the violators. For example, taxpayers are required to report their annual income on their tax returns.

3. Imposition by Regulation

Recordkeeping and reporting requirements are usually imposed by regulation, but some reporting requirements are informally imposed by the agency (e.g., by letter). Usually, in order to impose a recordkeeping or reporting requirement, the agency must find statutory authority, implicit or explicit. If an agency decides to impose a reporting or recordkeeping requirement by regulation, it must comply with the APA's rulemaking processes.

4. Imposition by Other Means

In *In re FTC Line of Business Report Litigation*, 595 F.2d 685 (D.C.Cir.1978), the court held that not all recordkeeping and reporting requirements must be imposed by regulation.

The Court held that the "Federal Trade Commission Act (FTC Act) provides a clear basis of authority for the Commission to issue orders requiring corporations to submit informational reports to the FTC."

5. The Paperwork Reduction Act

The Paperwork Reduction Act. 44 U.S.C.A. §§ 3501 *et seq.*, imposes limitations on an agency that seeks to impose reporting or recordkeeping requirements on 10 or more persons. However, the Act is subject to various exemptions. 44 U.S.C.A. § 3502(3).

a. Oversight Office

The Act requires agencies to establish offices that are required to oversee information collection. 44 U.S.C.A. § 3506(a)(2). When an agency proposes to collect information, the oversight office must review the request and evaluate the agency's asserted of need as well as the plan details. 44 U.S.C.A. § 3506(c)(1). In addition, the office must estimate the amount of burden imposed by the collection requirement. *Id.* If the agency does not proceed by rulemaking, the office must publish the collection requirement in the *Federal Register* and accept comments. 44 U.S.C.A. § 3506(c)(2). Once the comments are received, the office must certify that the information collection is necessary, is not duplicative of other information available to the agency, reduces the burden on small entities, is written understandably, is implemented consistently with existing reporting and recordkeeping practices, indicates the amount of time required to comply, and has been developed in a way designed to produce efficient and effective management and use of the information collected, uses effective and efficient statistical survey methodology, and uses information technology to reduce the burden and improve data quality, agency efficiency and responsiveness to the public. 44 U.S.C.A. § 3506(3).

b. OIRA Review

After the internal agency office conducts its review, the agency must submit its proposed collection requirement to the Office of Management and Budget's (OMB) Office of Information and Regulatory Affairs (OIRA). 44 U.S.C.A. § 3507(a)(1)(C). The proposal must then be published in the *Federal Register*, and OIRA must wait at least thirty days before approving the request and then must approve or disapprove the request within 60 days based on whether "the collection of information by the agency is necessary for the proper performance of the functions of the agency." 44 U.S.C.A. § 3508.

c. OIRA and Agency Rulemakings

If the agency opts to impose an information collection requirement by rule, OIRA participates in the rulemaking process by submitting com ments. 44 U.S.C.A. § 3507(d). If OIRA finds that the agency's response to its comments are "unreasonable," OIRA has 60 days to disapprove the rule. *Id.* However, when OIRA disapproves a request from an independent regulatory agency, the members can override the OIRA decision by majority vote. 44 U.S.C.A. § 3507(f). The agency head can circumvent these processes, and seek immediate approval, if he/she determines that there is an emergency. 44 U.S.C.A. § 3507(j).

d. Control Numbers

If OIRA approves an information collection request, OIRA provides a mandatory "control number" for the request. 44 U.S.C.A. § 3507(a)(3). If an information collection document does not contain a control number, or a required notice regarding the obligation to complete, those who refuse to comply cannot be penalized for failure to provide the requested information. 44 U.S.C.A. § 3512.

e. Paperwork Reduction Act Exemptions

The Paperwork Reduction Act does not apply to federal criminal investigations, to judicial actions to which the United States or an agency is a party, during an administrative action or investigation directed against specific persons, to functions performed by intelligence agencies, or by compulsory process under the Antitrust Civil Process Act or Section 13 of the Federal Trade Commission Improvements Act.

f. Judicial Review

An OIRA decision to approve an information collection is exempt from judicial review. 44 U.S.C.A. § 3507(d)(6).

E. SUBPOENAS AND THE FOURTH AMENDMENT

Early court decisions limited the power of administrative agencies to obtain information by subpoena. *See Federal Trade Commission v. American Tobacco Co.*, 264 U.S. 298, 44 S.Ct. 336, 68 L.Ed. 696 (1924). However, in *Oklahoma Press Publishing Co. v. Walling*, 327 U.S. 186, 66 S.Ct. 494, 90 L.Ed. 614 (1946), the Court held that an agency may subpoena information even if it lacks "probable cause." The Court found that a probable cause requirement "would stop much if not all of the investigation in the public interest at the threshold of the inquiry."

1. Requirement to "Particularly Describe"

In *Oklahoma Press*, instead of probable cause, the Court held that "[T]he Fourth [Amendment] . . . at most guards against abuse only by way of too much indefiniteness or breadth in the things required to be 'particularly described,' if also the inquiry is one the demanding agency is authorized by law to make and the materials specified are relevant. The gist of the protection is in the requirement, expressed in terms, that the disclosure shall not be unreasonable."

2. "Fishing Expeditions?"

United States v. Morton Salt Co., 338 U.S. 632, 70 S.Ct. 357, 94 L.Ed. 401 (1950), involved an agency's attempt to impose a reporting requirement on regulated entities. The Court rejected the company's assertion that the reporting requirement involved nothing more than a "fishing expedition" and therefore that production should not be required.

3. Whalen and Privacy Issues

In *Whalen v. Roe*, 429 U.S. 589, 97 S.Ct. 869, 51 L.Ed.2d 64 (1977), plaintiffs objected on privacy grounds to a New York statute that required physicians to submit drug prescription information to the state. Although the Court rejected plaintiffs' privacy claim, on the basis that only a few governmental officials had access to the information, the Court suggested that a privacy claim might limit reporting requirements in appropriate cases.

F. THE FIFTH AMENDMENT AND COMPELLED DISCLOSURES

In addition to Fourth Amendment constraints on governmental information collections, litigants sometimes challenge collections under the Fifth Amendment privilege against self-incrimination, which provides that no person "shall be compelled in any criminal case to be a witness against himself. . . . " U.S. Const. Amend V.

1. Application to Administrative Proceedings

Although the privilege against self-incrimination precludes incrimination in a criminal proceeding, testimony at civil or administrative proceedings can be criminally incriminating. In other words, statements made in administrative proceedings might be used to prosecute individuals in later criminal proceedings. As a result, the privilege applies to statements made in administrative proceedings which might be used against witnesses in subsequent or parallel criminal proceedings.

2. Prohibition Against "Testimonial" Self–Incrimination

In general, the privilege against self-incrimination protects witnesses only against compelled testimonial self-incrimination. In other words, witnesses can be protected against being forced to testify against themselves. The privilege generally does not protect witnesses against a requirement to produce documents.

3. Inapplicability to Corporations
In addition, the privilege only protects natural persons, and does not protect corporations or unincorporated associations.

4. Inapplicability to Corporate and Associational Documents
Given that the privilege against self-incrimination does not protect corporations, and applies only to testimony and not to documents, the privilege does not protect corporate books and records.

5. Inapplicability to "Required Records"
In *Shapiro v. United States*, 335 U.S. 1, 68 S.Ct. 1375, 92 L.Ed. 1787 (1948), the Court refused to apply the privilege to "required records" which the government requires an individual to keep "in order that there may be suitable information of transactions which are the appropriate subjects of government regulation and the enforcement of restrictions validly established."

6. Inapplicability to Other Documents
Because the privilege against self-incrimination protects only "testimony" and not documents, it does not protect incriminating documents held by an individual. *See United States v. Doe*, 465 U.S. 605, 104 S.Ct. 1237, 79 L.Ed.2d 552 (1984). This is true even for highly personal documents (e.g., a personal diary).

7. Registration Requirements
The privilege does apply when the government, or an agency of government requires an individual to register under circumstances which might be incriminating.

8. Incriminating Acts of Production
The privilege might apply to the production of documents when the "act" of production would, itself, be incriminating.

9. More on Incriminating Acts of Production
In *Braswell v. United States*, 487 U.S. 99, 108 S.Ct. 2284, 101 L.Ed.2d 98 (1988), the president of a company objected to a subpoena on the basis that the "act

of producing the records would incriminate him in violation of his Fifth Amendment privilege against self-incrimination." The Court held that, whether a "subpoena is addressed to the corporation, or as here, to the individual in his capacity as a custodian, a corporate custodian such as petitioner may not resist a subpoena for corporate records on Fifth Amendment grounds."

G. PARALLEL PROCEEDINGS

In some instances, when the government seeks information from companies or private individuals, it is pursuing both civil and criminal objectives. If the government is contemplating criminal charges, a potential defendant might object that it is inappropriate for the agency to use its civil powers to gather information as a predicate to a criminal prosecution.

1. *Dresser Industries* & Parallel Proceedings

In *Securities and Exchange Commission v. Dresser Industries, Inc.*, 628 F.2d 1368 (D.C.Cir.1980), Dresser Industries sought protection because it claimed that the SEC was conducting parallel civil and criminal investigations. The court rejected the challenge holding that, in "the absence of substantial prejudice to the rights of the parties involved, such parallel proceedings are unobjectionable under our jurisprudence."

2. *United States v. Kordel*

In *United States v. Kordel*, 397 U.S. 1, 90 S.Ct. 763, 25 L.Ed.2d 1 (1970), after the government used interrogatories against a corporation in a civil proceeding, plaintiffs claimed a violation of their Fifth Amendment privilege against compulsory self-incrimination when the interrogatory answers were used against them in a criminal proceeding. The Court rejected the claim noting that individuals who were concerned about incriminating themselves could have refused to testify in the civil proceeding based on their Fifth Amendment privilege against compulsory self-incrimination.

3. *Lasalle National Bank* & "Good Faith"

In *United States v. LaSalle National Bank*, 437 U.S. 298, 98 S.Ct. 2357, 57 L.Ed.2d 221 (1978), as part of a broad-based investigation of an individual, the Internal Revenue Service (IRS) subpoenaed records from a bank. The subpoena was challenged on the basis that the IRS was involved in a criminal investigation, and that it was improperly using a civil investigation to gather information for a criminal prosecution. Recognizing that the IRS code contains interrelated criminal and civil elements, and that the civil and criminal proceedings separate only when the IRS recommends a criminal prosecution to the Department of Justice, the Court held that the IRS could not issue a subpoena for *solely* criminal purposes. A subpoena will be upheld if two requirements are met: "First, the summons must be issued before the Service recommends to the Department of Justice that a criminal prosecution, which reasonably would relate to the subject matter of the summons, be undertaken. Second, the Service at all times must use the summons authority in good-faith pursuit of the congressionally authorized purposes of § 7602."

■ CHAPTER SIX: AGENCY STRUCTURE

A. INTRODUCTION

Administrative agencies raise basic questions about their power and their control by the political branches. In particular, questions arise about Congress's authority to delegate legislative power to the agency and its power to authorize agency courts to adjudicate disputes. In addition issues arise about the ability of Congress and the President to control agencies. This chapter takes up these topics in that order.

B. NON–DELEGATION

1. General Rule

The non-delegation doctrine derives from Article I's statement that "all legislative powers" granted to the federal government were to be vested in Congress. From this grew the idea that, as the People had allocated this power to Congress, it could not be delegated to other entities, such as administrative agencies. Of course, Congress has always delegated some duties to agencies. The modern test for those delegations asks whether Congress has provided an "intelligible principle" to govern the agency's action.

2. Leniency of the General Rule

The intelligible principle test is very easy for Congress to meet. The Court has only struck down two statutes as failing it, or violating the non-delegation doctrine more generally. Both of those cases, from 1935, featured exceptionally broad delegations without any real standards guiding the agency's action.

C. ADJUDICATION BY NON–ARTICLE III COURTS

Another type of delegation occurs when Congress provides that agencies, rather than Article III courts, should adjudicate cases arising under the statutes the agency administers.

1. Agency Courts Are Not Article III Courts

Agency courts are not Article III courts. Judges in agency courts ("administrative law judges" or "ALJs") are not selected with the advice and consent of the Senate, and the do not enjoy the salary and tenure protections enjoyed by Article III judges.

2. Early Doctrine: The Public/Private Right Distinction

In the 1856 case of *Murray's Lessee v. Hoboken Land Imp. Co.*, 59 U.S. (18 How.) 272, 15 L. Ed. 372 (1855), the Supreme Court distinguished between public and private rights. Since Congress created public rights, it could place their adjudication in non-Article III courts if it wished. Private rights, however, had to be litigated in Article III courts. Cases into the modern day continued to adhere to this distinction, which never fully disappeared and has in fact resurfaced in more recent years.

3. Balancing

In *Commodity Futures Trading Com'n v. Schor*, 478 U.S. 833, 106 S.Ct. 3245, 92 L.Ed.2d 675 (1986), the Court considered a complex scheme where a customer of a commodities broker could bring a statutorily-created "reparation" claim against the broker in an agency court, and the broker could bring a common law contract counterclaim against the customer in the same agency court.

a. Public/Private Rights

In the *Schor* test, the nature of the right as public or private remained relevant, but only as one factor.

b. The Essential Attributes of Judicial Power

The Court also considered whether the essential attributes of the Article III judicial power remained with Article III courts.

c. The Powers of the Agency Court

The Court also noted that the agency court did not exercise many of the powers normally exercised by Article III courts.

d. Congress' Motivations

Finally, *Schor* noted that Congress did not create the agency courts in that case in order to aggrandize or allocate power to itself, or otherwise to reduce the power of Article III courts. Rather, it created these courts in order to provide an efficient dispute resolution mechanism.

4. Stern v. Marshall

In a case from 2011, *Stern v. Marshall*, ___ U.S. ___, 131 S.Ct. 2594, 180 L.Ed.2d 475 (2011), the Court returned to a heavy reliance on the public/private rights distinction. However, *Stern* involved a bankruptcy court as the non-Article III adjudicator. The Court distinguished *Schor* on the ground that *Schor* involved an agency that, unlike the bankruptcy court, had substantive regulatory power over the subject matter.

D. THE LEGISLATIVE VETO AND OTHER METHODS OF CONGRESSIONAL CONTROL

1. Introduction

When Congress delegates broad power to agencies it often wishes to retain some supervisory power over how the agency uses its discretion. Congress has a variety of tools by which it can perform this supervision.

2. The Legislative Veto Explained

Congress has inserted provisions authorizing Congress to veto administrative action short of enacting an entirely new statute. Such "legislative vetoes" were found unconstitutional in 1983. However, other, more informal ways for Congress to influence agency action remain constitutional and widely used.

E. THE APPOINTMENT AND REMOVAL POWER

1. Introduction

One of the basic ways in which a President seeks to control agency action is by appointing heads of agencies. Questions arise, though, over whether Congress can restrict the President's powers in this regard.

2. Appointments Power Is Provided in Article II

Article II gives the President the power to nominate "Ambassadors . . . and all other Officers of the United States," but then goes on to state that

"Congress may by Law vest the Appointment of such inferior Officers, as they think proper, in the President alone, in the Courts of Law, or in the Heads of Departments."

3. Principal/Inferior Officer Distinction Based on Supervision and Scope of Duties

In *Morrison v. Olson*, 487 U.S. 654, 108 S.Ct. 2597, 101 L.Ed.2d 569 (1988) the Supreme Court determined that Special Prosecutors established under the now-defunct Special Prosecutor statute were inferior officers, and thus could be appointed by a panel of judges, rather than the President. The Court noted that the Special Prosecutor had limited duties, the office was of limited duration, and he was under the supervision of another official, the Attorney General.

4. The Removal Power in *Morrison*

In *Morrison v. Olson* the Court also considered the President's power to remove officials, as the Special Prosecutor statute was challenged on the ground that it allowed the Attorney General (who is subject to direct presidential direction) to remove the prosecutor only for "good cause." The Court upheld the "good cause" provision, stating that the President had the power to remove an officer only if denial of that power would make it impossible for him to carry out his constitutionally prescribed duties. The good cause removal provision was held to give the President adequate power to allow him to carry out those duties.

5. Limiting *Morrison*'s Reach

In a case from 2010 the Court did not give *Morrison* an expansive reading. Rather, it held that presidential power was unconstitutionally limited if *two* levels of good-cause protection separated him from an agency official.

■ CHAPTER SEVEN: PUBLIC ACCESS TO AGENCY PROCESSES

A. THE NEED FOR GOVERNMENT OPENNESS

For many years, government workings and government documents were largely shielded from public viewing and disclosure. However, over the last fifty years a series of statutes have made government more transparent.

B. THE FREEDOM OF INFORMATION ACT

In 1966, Congress passed the Freedom of Information Act (FOIA), which created a right of access to government information. FOIA is considered a "disclosure" statute–*i.e.*, it generally requires agencies to disclose information, rather than authorizing them to hold information in secret.

1. FOIA Is a Disclosure Statute

FOIA, section 552(a)(3), is widely regarded as a "disclosure" statute. In other words, it generally requires agencies to disclose information: "upon any request for records which reasonably describes such records and is made in accordance with published rules stating the time, place, fees (if any), and procedures to be followed," the agency must "make the records promptly available to any person."

2. FOIA Exemptions

Consistent with the idea that, despite the preference for disclosure some governmental information must be protected against disclosure, FOIA provides that nine different types of material are exempt from disclosure. The exemptions are: classified information; internal agency personnel rules and practices; information specifically exempted from disclosure by statute; private commercial or trade secret information; inter-agency or intra-agency privileged communications; personnel, medical, or similar files the disclosure of which would constitute a clearly unwarranted invasion of privacy; information compiled for law enforcement purposes; information related to reports for or by an agency involved in regulating financial institutions; and geological information concerning wells.

When a requested document contains both exempt and non-exempt material, the agency is required to disclose "reasonably segregable portion[s]" of the document. If an agency claims that particular documents are exempt, it must prepare an index of those documents and the reasons for non-disclosure, in order to allow a requester to challenge the denial.

3. Complying With FOIA

FOIA normally requires an administrative agency to decide within 20 working days whether to comply with a FOIA request. *See* 5 U.S.C.A. § 552(a)(6)(A)(i). Only rarely do agencies actually meet FOIA's time dead lines. When an agency does fail to meet a deadline, the requesting party may seek judicial review. 5 U.S.C.A. § 552(a)(6)(C). However, although a reviewing court should order immediate compliance absent "exceptional circumstances," most courts are patient, provided that the agency can demonstrate that it is proceeding diligently.

4. FOIA Fees

The original FOIA authorized agencies to impose "fair and equitable charges" for processing requests. In 1974, Congress limited the ability of agencies to impose fees, fearing that the fees would deter FOIA requests. Twelve years later, following a significant increase in the number of requests, Congress allowed agencies to recover the direct costs of search, duplication, and review associated with commercial requests. 5 U.S.C.A. § 552(a)(4)(A). The FOIA statute allows for a waiver of costs in certain cases.

5. Judicial Review

When a FOIA request is denied, the requester may seek judicial review and the burden of proof rests upon the agency (defendant) that is resisting disclosure. 5 U.S.C.A. § 552(a)(4)(B). Judicial review is *de novo* and the requestor may recover reasonable attorney's fees and costs if he/she prevails.

C. THE FEDERAL ADVISORY COMMITTEE ACT

The Federal Advisory Committee Act (FACA), 5 U.S.C.A. §§ 1–15, regulates the use of advisory committees. FACA provides for monitoring of the quantity of advisory committees and the amount of money spent by them.

1. Balance

FACA requires that the membership of advisory committees be "fairly balanced in terms of the points of view represented and the functions to be performed by the advisory committee." In other words, committees may not be stacked to favor particular perspectives.

2. Governmental Participation and Involvement

FACA also provides that an advisory committee meeting may not take place "except with the approval of, or with the advance approval of, a designated officer or employee of the Federal Government, and [except for Presidential advisory committees] with an agenda approved by such officer or employee."

3. FACA and Openness

FACA requires that "[e]ach advisory committee meeting shall be open to the public," and requires that "timely notice" of each meeting shall be published in the *Federal Register*. FACA also allows the public to appear and file statements with the committee, and requires committees to keep "detailed minutes of each meeting," the accuracy of which the chair of the committee must certify, and which must contain "a record of the persons present, a complete and accurate description of matter discussed and conclusions reached, and copies of all reports received, issued, or approved by the advisory committee." These records must be available for public inspection and copying.

4. FACA Enforcement

When FACA applies, but its provisions have not been satisfied, courts may (and often do) prohibit agencies from using information or recommendations derived from such committees.

D. GOVERNMENT IN THE SUNSHINE ACT

The Government in the Sunshine Act, 5 U.S.C.A. § 552b, requires that "every portion of every meeting of an agency shall be open to public observation." 5 U.S.C.A. § 552b(b). In enacting the law, Congress evinced its belief that "[b]y requiring important decisions to be made openly, [the law] will create better understanding of agency decisions."

1. Definition of "Agency"

Unlike the FOIA, the Sunshine Act only applies to agencies "headed by a collegial body composed of two or more individual members, a majority of whom are appointed to such position by the President with the advice and consent of the Senate, and any subdivision thereof authorized to act on behalf of the agency." 5 U.S.C.A. § 552b(a)(1). In other words, it applies to the SEC, FTC, FCC, FEC, and other similar agencies headed by collegial bodies, but does not apply to cabinet level agencies.

2. Definition of "Meeting"

The Sunshine Act only applies when there is meeting of a quorum of the members of the agency, and only when they are involved in "deliberations" that "determine or result in the joint conduct or disposition of official agency business." 5 U.S.C.A. § 552b(a)(2).

3. Exceptions

The Sunshine Act provides for closed meetings in certain specified situations.

4. Notice Requirement

The Sunshine Act mandates that agencies provide at least seven days notice of a meeting's subject matter, time, place, and whether the meeting will be open or closed. 5 U.S.C.A. § 552b(e)(1).

5. Judicial Review

The Sunshine Act's provisions are judicially enforceable and the agency is required to justify its actions. 5 U.S.C.A. § 552b(h). A plaintiff may be entitled to recover attorneys fees and litigation costs in an enforcement action, but the Act does not permit a court to invalidate agency action taken in violation of the Sunshine Act. 5 U.S.C.A. § 552b(h)(2).

■ CHAPTER EIGHT: ATTORNEY'S FEES

A. GENERAL RULE: EACH SIDE BEARS ITS OWN COSTS

Under the so-called "American Rule," each side generally bears its own legal costs. However, statutes sometimes alter this rule.

B. EQUAL ACCESS TO JUSTICE ACT (EAJA) ALLOWS SOME FEE RECOVERY

The EAJA provides for a private party to collect attorney's fees when litigating against the government when certain conditions are met.

1. The Private Party Must Have Prevailed

Under the EAJA a "prevailing party" may collect reasonable attorney's fees from the government in an adversary proceeding unless the agency position was "substantially justified" or special circumstances would render a fees award unjust.

2. Prevailing Status Is Determined Based on the Administrative Record

Whether the agency's position was "substantially justified" is to be determined based on the record of the administrative proceeding. 5 U.S.C. § 504.

3. Award May Be Limited if the Private Party Unreasonably Protracted the Proceedings

According to 5 U.S.C. § 504(a)(3), "The adjudicative officer of the agency may reduce the amount to be awarded, or deny an award, to the extent that the party during the course of the proceedings engaged in conduct which unduly and unreasonably protracted the final resolution of the matter in controversy."

4. Fees Available Against Excessive Demands

Fees are also available "if the demand by the agency is substantially in excess of the decision of the adjudicative officer and is unreasonable when compared with such decision." In such cases the party may recover fees and other expenses related to defending against the excessive demand. 5 U.S.C. § 504(a)(4).

5. Excessive Demand Fees Unavailable for Willful Violations or Bad Faith

Excessive demand fees are unavailable "if the party has committed a willful violation of law or otherwise acted in bad faith, or special circumstances make an award unjust." 5 U.S.C. § 504(a)(4).

6. Fees Include Witness Fees and Report Preparation

Under the EAJA fees include witness fees and report preparations. However, there are caps to the hourly rates at which fees and expenses may be recovered.

7. Prevailing Parties Limited by Size and Wealth

The EAJA defines "party" as individuals with a net worth of less than $2,000,000 and business associations with a net worth of less than $7,000,000 and less than 500 employees. These restrictions do not apply to tax-exempt parties.

8. Adversary Adjudication Includes Formal Adjudications

Under the EAJA an "adversarial adjudication" is an adjudication under 5 U.S.C. § 554—that is, a formal, on the record adjudication.

9. Voluntary Agency Provision of Formal Proceedings Does Not Trigger the EAJA

The EAJA applies only to adjudications where Congress intended it to apply. Thus, voluntary agency provision of a formal proceeding does not trigger its provisions.

10. Partial Prevailing Entitled Party to Some Fees

A party need not prevail entirely in order to claim at least some attorney's fees. A party receiving only a partial judgment may recover a proportionate fee award.

11. A Party May "Prevail" in the Absence of a Final Decision

Even without a final decision a party may still claim attorney's fees if it is able to show that the agency changed its position vis-à-vis the party, and that the adjudication was a substantial factor in that change.

12. Government's Justification Must Be Substantial

In order to avoid EAJA fees, the government must show that its position was "substantially justified." This requires simply that the position was justified to a point that would satisfy a reasonable person. However, in order to satisfy the requirement the government's position must be stronger than simply not meriting sanctions for frivolousness.

13. Government Position May Be Partially Justified

Some of the government's position may be substantially justified while others may not. In such a situation partial fees are appropriate.

Perspective

Administrative law can be a daunting topic for students first encountering it. Unless a student has first-hand experience with an administrative agency, the idea of an "administrator" "implementing" a statute seems abstract and remote, even if we have an intuitive sense of a bureaucracy that makes the day-to-day decisions that constitute government action.

But exactly what kinds of decisions do bureaucrats make? And what law governs the bureaucracy when they make them? Administrative law answers the first of these questions by dividing the universe of legally-binding administrative decisions into two, somewhat oversimplified categories. First, agencies promulgate regulations, or rules. A rule is a rough analog of a statute, in that it is a generally-applicable legal requirement. An example of a rule would be an Environmental Protection Agency requirement that manufacturers not dump a certain type of pollutant into waterways. Every other agency action is labeled an adjudication. As the name implies, adjudications are rough analogs to judicial decisions, in that it is a decision about the legal rights and obligations of a particular individual, based on that individual's particular facts. An example of an adjudication would be a decision by the EPA that a particular manufacturer had violated the law (either a statute or an agency rule) by dumping a particular quantity of a particular pollutant into a particular waterway.

Of course, many agency actions do not fall easily within these two categories. Agencies collect information, investigate general economic and social conditions and the conduct of particular parties, advise Congress, the President and private parties about what the law is or what it should be, and perform a myriad of tasks in support of these and other general functions. But note that these latter tasks do not involve the imposition of legal obligations. By contrast, rules and adjudications do, and for that reason they are of primary interest to students of administrative law.

Now, to the second question: what law governs the agency when it promulgates a rule or performs an adjudication? Of course, the authorizing statute has a lot to say about how the agency acts. By "authorizing statute," we mean nothing more than the statute that establishes the underlying congressional policy on a given issue and authorizes the agency to implement that policy. Thus, the Clean Water Act establishes a federal policy that the disposal of pollutants into federal waters should be controlled in order to clean up those waterways, via a system of emissions permitting, and authorizes the EPA to issue those permits and to promulgate regulations governing that permitting system. Thus, one of the main questions administrative law concerns itself with is the degree to which courts can scrutinize whether the agency, in promulgating a rule or performing an adjudication, has strayed from the authority Congress gave it.

But just as important as the agency's fidelity to the substantive law is the agency's use of appropriate procedures. In general, when government imposes legal duties on individuals, it has to act by means of some process which is at least minimally fair. This is especially true when government singles out an individual for imposition of a legal duty: recall the panoply of procedural protections (a jury trial, a right to counsel, etc.) we require before government can convict someone of a crime and imprison him. Thus, when an agency adjudicates—i.e., when it singles an individual out for imposition of a legal obligation (even one not as serious as a prison term) we require, as a matter of constitutional right under the Due Process clause, that the agency provide some minimal level of fair procedure. Often the authorizing statute provides such a procedure, which leads to many cases in which a court considers whether those statutorily-mandated procedures satisfy the Due Process clause.

Sometimes, however, the statute will not set forth any particular procedures. In that case, an agency must follow the Administrative Procedure Act ("APA"). The APA is a crucially important statute for administrative law; indeed, much of your course will be taken up with studying it. The APA, enacted in 1946, was designed to be the fundamental law governing how administrative agencies promulgate rules and perform adjudications, and specifying the law governing judicial review of those agency actions. It is important to note that the APA provides the default rules for administrative agencies to follow. If the authorizing statute sets forth the procedure the agency must follow, or the rules for seeking judicial review of the agency's action, then it is those procedures and rules, and not the APA's, which govern. But because many statutes are silent on these issues, and because those that are not silent often take their cues from the APA, that statute remains centrally important to administrative law.

Surprisingly, the APA provides procedures to be followed for adjudications only when the agency is required by statute to engage in relatively formal, trial-type adjudicative procedures. Informal adjudications, which constitute the vast majority of agency adjudications, are tested only against the requirements of the Due Process clause (assuming, of course, that the authorizing statute does not itself prescribe a procedure).

Rulemaking procedures proceed along a different track. Early in the 20th century it was established that rulemaking procedures were not subject to the requirements of the Due Process clause. Thus, the only procedures required of an agency when it engages in rulemaking are found in the authorizing statute or the APA. Often, the authorizing statute is silent on the types of rulemaking procedures the agency is required to use, thus leaving the APA's procedures. Again unlike with adjudications, the APA provides procedures for both formal and informal rulemaking. As you'll see, formal rulemakings under the APA must follow most of the trial-type procedures the APA prescribes for formal adjudications. Unlike with adjudications, however, the APA also provides procedures for informal rulemaking. These latter procedures are called "notice and comment" procedures because in essence they require the agency to provide public "notice" that the agency is considering promulgating a rule, and to offer the public a meaningful opportunity to "comment" on the proposed rule.

Beyond questions about whether an agency's action faithfully followed the statute authorizing it to act, and whether the agency followed appropriate procedures, administrative law concerns itself with a more fundamental question: the constitutional status of administrative agencies. Administrative agencies are not mentioned in the Constitution. Under our system, Congress makes the law by legislating, the President enforces that law, and courts adjudicate disputes under that law. Agencies disrupt this traditional thinking in several ways. First, they combine all of these functions: by promulgating rules, they essentially legislate. Of course, they also investigate and enforce. Finally, they adjudicate disputes arising under their authorizing statutes. One of administrative law's basic questions concerns the need to control this concentration of power in one entity, a concentration that runs counter to basic American separation of powers theory. A second constitutional problem arises with the problem of control. While most agencies are under the direct control of the President, in the sense that he can dismiss at will the top officials of that agency, many of the most important agencies in our system are led by administrators who have some degree of independence from the White House. For example, the Federal Reserve Board is led by officials who enjoy this sort of independence. The constitutional justifications for this "headless fourth branch of government" constitute another major issue for administrative law scholars.

As you might expect given the difficulty of these questions, scholars, judges, and lawyers have all developed theories to justify the existence of the administrative state. These theories are important for students because courts have embraced them, at various times and to various degrees, and have crafted doctrine with those theories in mind. Some theorists have focused on fair procedure, and have justified agency action on the ground that it is the product of a fundamentally fair process. These theorists have stressed the procedural protections of the APA and the Due Process clause, and have looked skeptically at attempts to streamline that process. Other theorists have argued that agency action is legitimate because the problems agencies confront are technical, rather than political, ones. These theorists focus on the technical expertise specialized agencies have over regulatory problems (e.g., the EPA over environmental quality issues), and defend agency action as technically competent responses to those problems. These theorists, as you might expect, are less concerned about procedural fairness; indeed, they favor streamlining those procedures in order to make agencies able to respond to problems more quickly and easily. Finally, some theorists defend agency action on the grounds that it is ultimately responsive to control from democratically-elected officials, usually the President. These theorists believe that agency action is political, rather than technical, but disagree with the proceduralists over the proper response. For these theorists, agency action is best legitimated by making agency officials responsive to the President, who, as a politician, can be expected to respond to popular demands.

No one of these theories has ever fully explained administrative law; today, as well as yesterday, administrative law responds to all of them, to differing degrees as the theories rise and fall in acceptance. As you study administrative law, keep these theories in the back of your mind and ask yourself how the doctrines you study reflect them.

PREPARING FOR THE EXAM

As noted above, administrative law can be a daunting subject for a student. However, keeping a few basic principles in mind will help make it more manageable, and will give you the structure you need in order to organize what you will be studying.

First, administrative law draws a basic distinction between substance and process. Substance deals with the degree to which the agency has faithfully applied its authorizing statute—the degree, in other words, to which the agency has done what Congress wanted. By contrast, process deals with the extent to which the agency has followed procedures required by law (either the Due Process clause, the authorizing statute, or the APA). When agency action is challenged in court, it is usually (although not always) because the agency has allegedly strayed either from the policy Congress set in the statute or from the procedure it was required to follow.

Second, if the claim is procedural, keep in mind the distinction between rulemaking and adjudication. Rulemaking and adjudications are governed by different procedures. Adjudications must always comply with the Due Process clause, in addition to whatever procedures may be required in the authorizing statute or the APA. By contrast, Due Process does not impose any requirements on rulemaking procedure. Thus, all that is procedurally required when an agency does a rulemaking is that it comply with either the authorizing statute or the APA.

Third, if the claim is that the agency failed to follow the substance of the congressional policy embodied in the statute, keep in mind that an important question will be the standard of review the court will use to review the agency's argument that it complied with the statute. The Supreme Court has erected a complex jurisprudence with differing standards of review, depending on the type of authority Congress gave to the agency. If the challenge is a substantive one, keep in mind that you will need to consider this standard of review question before deciding which side should prevail.

Fourth, keep in mind the rules about whether and under what conditions the plaintiff can seek judicial review at all. Article III of the Constitution and the APA both establish a complex set of hurdles a plaintiff must surmount before getting a court to even consider her claims against the agency. Often these rules will affect who can seek judicial review and whether review can be sought at an early stage of the agency's action or whether the plaintiff will have to await further agency action.

Fifth, keep in mind other possible claims that might be made against an agency. Plaintiffs have rights against agencies that go beyond how agencies perform rulemaking and adjudication. For example, the Freedom of Information Act gives individuals rights to seek information the agency possesses. Sometimes a fact pattern will implicate one of these rights.

Finally, be aware that your professor may also discuss the administrative law of a given state. States have bureaucracies just like the federal government, and have developed their own administrative laws and doctrines to control them. This book focuses on federal administrative law. While most state administrative law is similar, it is sometimes quite different, and at the very least is usually different in its details.

HOW TO USE THIS BOOK

This book can be helpful as you study administrative law. To get the full benefit, however, you should use it as a supplement to, rather than a substitute for, your course reading. Use it after you do your required course reading, as a summary of the basic rules reflected in the cases and the APA. You can also use it as a resource when preparing your own outline, as you prepare for your exam. Used in this way, this book can remind you of basic rules you may have overlooked, and can show you how the rules fit together. Its internal divisions—for example, between judicial review of the substance of the agency action and its procedural regularity—can remind you of how your course is structured. But note that this book cannot, by its very nature, provide all the nuance and complexity that will be demanded of you on the exam. Think of this book as a skeleton of the course. By doing your required reading and thinking about what is discussed in class, you can put the meat on that skeleton.

CHAPTER ONE

Rulemaking

A. THE RULEMAKING PROCESS

This chapters focuses on the process by which agencies make "legislative" rules. As we shall see, agencies usually have two options for making rules: formal rulemaking processes (the equivalent of trial-type procedures); & informal rulemaking procedures (which utilize so-called "notice and comment" procedures). 5 U.S.C.A. § 553. Some statutes may also impose "hybrid" procedures, which involve a cross between formal and informal rulemaking procedures.

B. RULEMAKING INITIATION

The initiation of rulemaking proceedings can come about in a number of different ways. First, the agency may decide on its own to initiate a rulemaking. Second, the agency may be commanded to begin a rulemaking by Congress. Finally, the impetus for rulemaking may come from interested persons or regulated entities, or from pressure applied by the executive or legislative branches.

1. Petitions for Rulemaking

One way that rulemaking can be initiated is by the filing of a petition requesting a rulemaking. The APA provides that "[e]ach agency shall give an interested person the right to petition for issuance, amendment, or repeal of a rule." 5 U.S.C.A. § 553(e). The APA also mandates that "[p]rompt notice shall be given of the denial in whole or in part of a written application, petition, or other request of an interested person made in connection with any agency proceeding" and "the notice shall be accompanied by a brief statement of the grounds for denial." Id. § 555(e). Under section 555, an agency cannot ignore a petition for rulemaking since it must give "prompt notice . . . of the denial" and must accompany the notice with "a brief statement of the grounds for the denial." Thus, filing a petition is a way to force some action out of an otherwise reluctant agency.

2. Compelling Agency Action

Section 551(13) of the APA defines "agency action" to include "failure to act," and this definition of agency action applies to the judicial review chapter of the APA. 5 U.S.C.A. § 701(b)(2). Section 706, which addresses the scope of judicial review of agency action, specifically provides that "[t]he reviewing court shall compel agency action unlawfully withheld or unreasonably delayed." 5 U.S.C.A. § 706(1). Courts rarely compel agency action except, perhaps, when Congress has established an explicit deadline by statute. But even when Congress has imposed a deadline, courts may not regard it as enforceable.

3. Denial of Petitions

If an agency denies a petition for rulemaking, the denial constitutes a reviewable action. However, the scope of review may be limited by the "arbitrary, capricious . . . abuse of discretion" standard of judicial review. *See* 5 § U.S.C.A. § 706(2)(a). In a leading case on the question, the D.C. Circuit has stated that such denials are reviewed very deferentially. *See American Horse Protection Ass'n v. Lyng*, 812 F.2d 1 (D.C. Cir. 1987).

C. EXEMPTIONS FROM RULEMAKING

Section 553 of the APA governs rulemaking and provides for informal rulemaking by "notice and comment" procedures, and formal rulemaking (trial-type proceedings) under sections 556 and 557.

1. Notice & Comment Exceptions

APA Section 553 exempts several types of rulemaking from some or all procedural requirements. That section exempts rulemakings concerning "a military or foreign affairs function of the United States" or "a matter relating to agency management or personnel or to public property, loans, grants, benefits, or contracts" from all of section 553's requirements. 5 U.S.C.A. § 553(a).

2. Additional Exceptions

Section 553 also exempts from the actual rulemaking process itself "interpretative rules, general statements of policy, or rules of agency organization, procedure, or practice" and "when the agency for good cause finds . . . that notice and public procedure thereon are impracticable, unnecessary, or contrary to the public interest." 5 U.S.C.A. § 553(b). In addition, the requirement that rules be published at least 30 days before their effective date does not apply to "a substantive rule which grants or recognizes an exemption or relieves a restriction; interpretative rules and statements of policy; or as otherwise provided by the agency for good cause found" 5 U.S.C.A. § 553(d).

3. Publication of Exempt Rules

Even if a rule is exempt from rulemaking requirements under Section 553, publication may be required. Section 552, the Freedom of Information Act (FOIA), imposes a requirement that "substantive rules of general applicability adopted as authorized by law" and "each amendment, revision, or repeal of the foregoing" be published in the *Federal Register* "for the guidance of the public." If an agency fails to comply with Section 552, then affected individuals may not be adversely affected by the rule unless they have actual notice of the rule.

D. TYPES OF RULEMAKING PROCESSES

As previously noted, rulemaking can fit into one of three categories: informal, formal, and hybrid. Although the APA only provides for formal and informal rulemaking processes, Congress sometimes imposes additional requirements (hybrid procedures) in addition to or in place of notice and comment procedures.

E. INFORMAL RULEMAKING

Informal rulemaking, also referred to as "notice and comment rulemaking," requires the agency to provide notice in the *Federal Register* to institute rulemaking. 5 U.S.C.A. § 553 (b). After such notice the agency is required to "give interested persons an opportunity to participate in the rulemaking through submission of written data, views, or arguments with or without opportunity for oral presentation." 5 U.S.C.A. § 553 (c). This opportunity constitutes the "comment" part of "notice and comment" rulemaking. This provision has generally been interpreted to allow the agency to refuse to allow oral presentations, and instead to require interested parties to submit comments in writing or electronically. Congress rarely requires agencies to utilize formal rulemaking procedures, contained in APA sections 556–57, which essentially require agencies to create rules using trial-type procedures.

1. Choice Between Formal and Informal Procedures

In general, agencies use "informal" rather than "formal" rulemaking procedures, and in most cases neither Congress nor the courts require agencies to use formal procedures.

a.   Statutes Requiring Rules to be Made "On the Record."

In *United States v. Allegheny–Ludlum Steel Corp.*, 406 U.S. 742, 92 S.Ct. 1941, 32 L.Ed.2d 453 (1972), the Court held that formal rulemaking procedures, as set forth in 5 U.S.C. §§ 556 and 557 of the APA, are required only "[w]hen rules are required by statute to be made on the record after opportunity for an agency hearing. . . . " As a result, a statute providing only that rules must be made "after hearing" does not impose formal procedures.

b.   Requirement of a "Hearing"

Allegheny's holding was reinforced in *United States v. Florida East Coast Railway Co.*, 410 U.S. 224, 93 S.Ct. 810, 35 L.Ed.2d 223 (1973).   In that case, the Court held that the word "hearing" in the Interstate Commerce Act did "not necessarily embrace either the right to present evidence orally and to cross-examine opposing witnesses, or the right to present oral argument to the agency's decisionmaker." Rather, the Court suggested that, except in unusual cases, formal rulemaking requirements are triggered only when Congress uses the actual words from Section 553, "on the record after opportunity for agency hearing."

c.   Rationale

The Court's decision to limit the situations in which formal rulemaking is required is generally thought to reflect the awkwardness of such formality in a multi-party rulemaking process based on broad social facts rather than facts unique to a particular party.

2.   Notice Requirements

The APA requires that informal rulemaking proceedings be commenced by a "general notice of proposed rulemaking . . . published in the Federal Register." 5 U.S.C.A. § 553(b). These notices are usually abbreviated as "NOPRs" (notice of proposed rulemakings). Technically, a *Federal Register* notice is not required if persons subject to the rule "are named or either personally served or otherwise have actual notice [of the rulemaking] in accordance with law," but agencies routinely publish notices in the *Federal Register* and the government's regulation internet site, regulations.gov. *Id.*; see http://www.regulations.gov/#!home.

a.   Practical Application of the Notice Requirement

By publishing a NOPR in the *Federal Register*, agencies provide "constructive" notice of a rulemaking process to interested parties, and this notice is valid even against those who are not involved in rulemaking process. For this reason, lawyers and companies that deal with regulatory areas routinely monitor notices published in the *Federal Register*. Sometimes, they do this through trade associations, which monitor the *Federal Register* on a daily basis. Large clients, or those with a lot at stake, hire their own lawyers to monitor agency announcements. In addition, information can be obtained from loose-leaf reporter services and other trade publications, which also monitor the *Federal Register* and publish information about proposed rulemakings. Access to the *Federal Register* is now available online. See https://www.federalregister.gov/.

b. NOPR Requirements

A NOPR must include the "time, place, and nature" of the public proceedings. 5 U.S.C.A. § 553(b)(1). The notice is designed to allow interested persons to participate in the rulemaking process by indicating the type of rule involved, the time during which the agency will receive written comments, and instructions concerning where to file the comments. An agency must also indicate the legal authority under which the rule is proposed and "either the terms or substance of the proposed rule or a description of the subjects and issues involved." *Id.* § 553(b)(3).

c. Additional Information

In many instances, agencies publish additional information in their NOPRs. For example, agencies may publish the text of the proposed rule. They also might publish a "preamble" which provides a background to the rulemaking and describes what the rule is intended to do. Sometimes, agencies publish this information voluntarily, but sometimes their governing statutes require the publication of such information.

d. Additional Judicially Imposed Requirements

Some courts have imposed expanded notice requirements for NOPRs. The APA provides that notice must be "sufficient to fairly apprise interested persons of the issues involved, so that they may present responsive data or argument." Legislative History of the Administrative Procedure Act, S. Doc. No. 248, 79th Cong., 2d Sess. 200 (1946). As a result, in cases like *Portland Cement Association v. Ruckelshaus*, 486 F.2d 375 (D.C. Cir. 1973), *cert. denied* 417 U.S. 921, 94 S.Ct. 2628, 41 L.Ed.2d 226 (1974), courts have required agencies to identify in their NOPRs the data and methodology of scientific evidence on which they are relying. Some courts continue to impose similar requirements, despite the Supreme Court's holding in *Vermont Yankee Nuclear Power Corp. v. National Resources Defense Council*, 435 U.S. 519, 98 S.Ct. 1197, 55 L.Ed.2d 460

(1978), that courts should not impose procedural requirements on agencies beyond those in the APA or the agency's governing statute.

e. Notice and Changes in a Rule's Text

Sometimes, as an agency receives comments on a proposed rule, it alters its views as well as the text of a rule. If the final rule is not a "logical outgrowth" of the NOPR, the agency should (at least in theory) issue a new NOPR.

f. More on the "Logical Outgrowth" Test

In *American Medical Association v. United States*, 887 F.2d 760, 767–68 (7th Cir. 1989), the court held that the critical issue under the "logical outgrowth" rule is whether the NOPR put interested parties on notice that "their interests [were] 'at stake.' " As a result, "the relevant inquiry is whether or not potential commentators would have known that an issue in which they were interested was 'on the table' and was to be addressed by a final rule. From this perspective it is irrelevant whether the proposal contained in the NOPR was favorable to a particular party's interests; the obligation to comment is not limited to those *adversely* affected by a proposal. '[A]pproval of a practice in a proposed rule may properly alert interested parties that the practice may be disapproved in the final rule in the event of adverse comments.' "

3. Opportunity for Comment

APA Section 553(c) requires agencies to provide interested persons an opportunity to comment on NOPRs by the "through submission of written data, views, or arguments."

a. Scope of the Requirement

The APA is not specific regarding the meaning of the comment requirement. However, the NOPR must indicate the place where comments should be sent and the submission date. The APA does not require that interested parties be give an opportunity for an oral presentation or a hearing, but it does require that final rules be published 30 days prior to their effective date. *Id.* § 553(d). Many agencies provide for far more than 30 days, and frequently grant requests to extend the comment period. Extensions, like the original NOPR, are also announced in the *Federal Register*.

b. Additional Legislatively Imposed Requirements

Congress has authority to alter the comment period, and it has done so in some acts. For example, in The Safe Drinking Water Act, Congress imposed a 60–day comment period for certain types of rules. 42 U.S.C.A. § 300g–1(b)(2)(B).

c. Electronic Commenting

Responding to the growth of electronic communications, many agencies now permit comments to be submitted electronically, and also allow interested parties to review the comments of other interested parties electronically. *See, e.g.,* Bridget C.E. Dooling, "Legal Issues in E–Rulemaking," 63 *Admin. L. Rev.* 893 (2011).

d. *Ex Parte* Communications

Unlike adjudicative proceedings and formal rulemakings, where *ex parte* contacts with agency decisionmakers are severely circumscribed, outside contacts are normally permitted during the notice-and-comment rulemaking process. However, Congress can prohibit *ex parte* contacts, and some agencies have chosen to do so on their own.

e. *Ex Parte* Contacts Involving Conflicting Claims

In *Sangamon Valley Television Corp. v. United States,* 269 F.2d 221 (D.C. Cir. 1959), the court held that due process prohibits *ex parte* contacts when rulemaking involves "conflicting private claims to a valuable privilege." That case involved litigation about television licenses by competing parties, and the court held that due process prohibited one of the parties from making *ex parte* contacts.

f. Other Limits on *Ex Parte* Contacts

In *Home Box Office v. Federal Communications Commission,* 567 F.2d 9 (D.C. Cir. 1977), *ex parte* contacts were made regarding a rulemaking after the notice and comment period had closed, and therefore were not reflected in the rulemaking record. The court expressed concern that, if "actual positions were not revealed in public comments, as this statement would suggest, and, further, if the Commission relied on these apparently more candid private discussions in framing the final . . . rules, then the elaborate public discussion in these dockets has been reduced to a sham." The Court concluded that the *ex parte* contacts must be included— otherwise the "full administrative record" would not be revealed: "If *ex parte* contacts nonetheless occur, we think that any written document or a summary of any oral communication must be placed in the public file established for each rulemaking docket immediately after the communication is received so that interested parties may comment thereon." However, soon after *Home Box Office* the same court interpreted that case as implicating "conflicting private claims to a valuable privilege," and thus as not expanding the *Sangamon Valley* rule. *Action for Children's Television v. Federal Communications Commission,* 564 F.2d 458, 477 (D.C.

Cir. 1977). (Note that, despite the reporter volume numbers, *Act for Children's Television* was decided after *Home Box Office*.)

g. Contacts by White House Officials

In *Sierra Club v. Costle*, 657 F.2d 298 (D.C. Cir. 1981), the court recognized that agency officials could meet with White House officials about proposed rules. In permitting such contacts, the court noted the "basic need of the President and his White House staff to monitor the consistency of executive agency regulations with Administration policy." However, the court noted that "that there may be instances where the docketing of conversations between the President or his staff and other Executive Branch officers or rulemakers may be necessary to ensure due process." These include situations when "such conversations directly concern the outcome of adjudications or quasi-adjudicatory proceedings." Nevertheless, the court held that "in the absence of any further Congressional requirements . . . it was not unlawful . . . for EPA not to docket a face-to-face policy session involving the President and EPA officials during the post-comment period, since EPA makes no effort to base the rule on any 'information or data' arising from that meeting." Moreover, the court noted that "[w]here the President himself is directly involved in oral communications with Executive Branch officials, Article II considerations combined with the strictures of *Vermont Yankee* require that courts tread with extraordinary caution in mandating disclosure beyond that already required by statute."

4. Statement of Basis and Purpose

After receiving comments from interested persons, Section 553(c) requires agencies, "after consideration of the relevant matter presented, [to] incorporate in the rules adopted a concise general statement of their basis and purpose." This requirement was designed "to enable the public to obtain a general idea of the purpose of, and a statement of the basis and justification for, the rules," rather than "an elaborate analysis of rules or of the detailed considerations upon which they are based." Legislative History of the Administrative Procedure Act, *supra*, at 225. Some so-called preambles to rules can be very long because agencies hope, or believe, that longer preambles will better enable their rules to survive judicial review.

F. FORMAL RULEMAKING PROCEDURES

Formal rulemakings are governed by Sections 556 and 557 of the APA. Those procedures generally allow oral presentations in front of either an administrative law judge or the head or heads of the agency. 5 U.S.C.A. § 556(b).

1. Presiding Officer

The person(s) presiding over the hearing enjoys powers over procedures typically associated with a judicial proceeding, including the power to administer oaths, issue subpoenas, and take, or cause to be taken, depositions. 5 U.S.C.A. § 556. Section 553(c) reads: After notice required by this section, the agency shall give interested persons an opportunity to participate in the rulemaking through submission of written data, views, or arguments with or without opportunity for oral presentation. After consideration of the relevant matter presented, the agency shall incorporate in the rules adopted a concise general statement of their basis and purpose. When rules are required by statute to be made on the record after opportunity for an agency hearing, sections 556 and 557 of this title apply instead of this subsection. 5 U.S.C.A. § 553.

(West) Section 555 discusses issuing subpoenas and powers of the agency holding the hearing (I think).

2. Oral Hearings

In formal proceedings, "a party is entitled to present his case or defense by oral or documentary evidence, to submit rebuttal evidence, and to conduct such cross-examination as may be required for a full and true disclosure of the facts." 5 U.S.C.A. § 556(d). However, that section also states "In rule making . . . an agency may, when a party will not be prejudiced thereby, adopt procedures for the submission of all or part of the evidence in written form." *Id.* The seeming contradiction is resolved when one realizes that Section 556 governs both formal *rulemaking* and formal *adjudication*, with the provision for written submission applicable to rulemaking.

3. *Ex Parte* Contacts

Section 557(d) restricts *ex parte* contacts from persons outside the agency in the course of a formal rulemaking. If such communications are made, the presiding officer is required to place on the rulemaking record any written *ex parte* communications, and summaries of any oral *ex parte* communications. A party who makes such a communication risks an adverse ruling on the merits of the issue. 5 U.S.C.A. § 557(d)(1)(D).

G. HYBRID RULEMAKING PROCEDURES

Sometimes agencies create rules using "hybrid" procedures—essentially a combination of informal and formal rulemaking procedures. In some instances, agencies choose to use hybrid procedures. In others, Congress mandates that agencies include additional procedures in addition to, or instead of, APA-mandated procedures.

1. **Judicially–Imposed Hybrid Procedures**

   In *Vermont Yankee Nuclear Power Corp. v. Natural Resources Defense Council, Inc.*, 435 U.S. 519, 98 S.Ct. 1197, 55 L.Ed.2d 460 (1978), the Court considered whether courts can impose hybrid rulemaking procedures on an agency. In that case, the Natural Resources Defense Council (NRDC) argued that, if it was denied the opportunity to engage in discovery and cross-examination as part of a rulemaking process, it would not have a "meaningful opportunity" to participate in the proceedings. The appellate court agreed and held that the agency was required to use "adequate" procedures. The United States Supreme Court reversed, holding that, while "[a]gencies are free to grant additional procedural rights in the exercise of their discretion . . . reviewing courts are generally not free to impose them if the agencies have not chosen to grant them." The Court concluded that such additional procedures were inconsistent with the Administrative Procedure Act, which struck a balance between the forces militating for more and for less elaborate procedures. Finally, the Court expressed concern that judicially-mandated requirements might force agencies "to conduct all rulemaking proceedings with the full panoply of procedural devices normally associated only with adjudicatory hearings," in order to ensure that a court would not find the process insufficient.

2. **Congressionally–Imposed Hybrid Procedures**

   Even though *Vermont Yankee* precludes courts from imposing hybrid rulemaking requirements on administrative agencies, there is nothing to prevent Congress from doing so. In a number of statutes, Congress has imposed additional requirements on the rulemaking process.

   a. **National Environmental Policy Act**

      Under the National Environmental Policy Act (NEPA), Congress requires agencies to prepare Environmental Impact Statements (EIS) before engaging in activities (including rulemaking) that may have a significant effect on the human environment. *See* 42 U.S.C.A. § 4332(2)(c). The EIS requirement forces agencies to detail how a proposed action might affect the environment, as well as to discuss the effects of proposed actions. NEPA does not require agencies to respond in any particular way to the EIS. It simply requires that an EIS be prepared as part of the rulemaking process.

   b. **Regulatory Flexibility Act**

      The Regulatory Flexibility Act requires agencies to create a Regulatory Flexibility Analysis (RFA) whenever a rule may have a significant economic impact on a substantial number of small businesses, organizations, or governments. 5 U.S.C.A. § 601 *et seq.* The analysis must accompany the proposed rule and state the reasons for the proposal, a statement of the rule's objectives and legal basis, a description of the affected small entities and the reporting and recordkeeping requirements, an identification of other federal rules that may overlap or conflict with the proposed rule, and a description of any significant regulatory alternatives that would accomplish the stated objectives but minimize the impact on small entities. After the comment period, when the agency issues the final rule, it must include a "final" RFA that describes the comments received, provides a response, and explains why alternatives (that might have reduced the impact on small entities) were accepted or rejected. Courts may review agency compliance with the Act's requirements.

c. Paperwork Reduction Act

The Paperwork Reduction Act of 1980, 44 U.S.C.A. §§ 3501 *et seq.*, requires agencies to engage in a notice and comment procedure prior to imposing any reporting or recordkeeping requirement on persons. The Act applies regardless of whether the information is to be reported to a federal agency or to the public. The Act also gives the Office of Information and Regulatory Affairs (OIRA), part of the Office of Management and Budget (OMB), power to approve or disapprove the rules.

d. Unfunded Mandates Reform Act of 1995

Title II of the Unfunded Mandates Reform Act of 1995, Pub. L. No. 104–4, 109 Stat. 48, entitled "Regulatory Accountability and Reform," requires federal agencies, before promulgating either a proposed or final regulation that would include a "mandate" resulting in costs over $100 million annually, to prepare an analysis of the regulation's effect. As part of its analysis, the agency must "identify and consider a reasonable number of regulatory alternatives," and must "select the least costly, most cost-effective or least burdensome alternative that achieves the objectives of the rule." 2 U.S.C.A. § 1535(a).

e. Congressional Review of Agency Rulemaking Act

In 1996, Congress enacted the Congressional Review of Agency Rulemaking Act, Pub. L. 104–121 (codified at 5 U.S.C.A. §§ 801–808). The statute mandates that agencies delay the effective date of rules for 60 days, except in certain circumstances, in order to give Congress the opportunity to enact a resolution rejecting the regulations. The resolution can only become law if signed by the President or passed by a two-thirds majority over his veto.

f.   Data Quality Act

The Data Quality Act (DQA), Treasury and General Government Appropriations Act for Fiscal Year 2001, Pub. L. No. 106–554, § 515 (2001), requires agencies to issue guidelines that ensure and maximize the "quality," "objectivity," "utility," and "integrity" of information that they disseminate, to establish an administrative process that allows affected persons to seek and obtain correction of information that does not meet those benchmarks, and to report yearly to the Office of Management and Budget (OMB) concerning the receipt and resolution of complaints. OMB is required to guide agencies regarding the content of their guidelines. In 2004, OMB promulgated guidelines that require regulatory agencies to hire independent scientists to peer review most of the scientific information disseminated by the government. Peer review applies both to scientific information that the government relies on to support a regulation as well as information used in government reports and on government web sites.

3.   Presidentially Imposed Procedures

In addition to congressionally imposed hybrid requirements, various presidents have imposed additional requirements.

a.   Executive Order 12291 (Cost–Benefit Analysis)

In 1981, by executive order (EO), President Ronald Reagan required administrative agencies to assess the benefits and costs of proposed and final "major" rules. Exec. Order No. 12291, 3 C.F.R. § 127 (1982), 5 U.S.C.A. § 601 (1988). The EO defined "major" rules as those having an annual economic impact of $100 million or more on the economy or one with other significant effects on individuals, businesses, governments, or the economy. Although OIRA was authorized to provide input on proposed rules, the EO did not give it the power to disapprove a proposed rule. However, the EO did prohibit agencies from promulgating any regulation when its benefits did not exceed its costs (absent other statutory authority).

b.   Extension of Cost–Benefit Analysis

In addition to signing Exec. Order No. 12291, President Reagan issued subsequent orders requiring executive agencies to consider the impact of their actions on various other matters (e.g., federalism, property and trade, and the family).

c. Executive Order 12866

In 1993, President Bill Clinton issued Executive Order 12866, which replaced Executive Order 12291, but kept most of the prior order's requirements.

However, it replaced the term "major rule" with the term "significant action," and it likewise required OIRA to oversee agency compliance.

d. Executive Order 13211

In 2001, President George W. Bush issued an executive order, E.O. 13211, 66 Fed. Reg. 28355 (2001), which required agencies to include Statements of Energy Effects (SEE) when they propose significant regulatory action which could have a significant adverse effect on the supply, distribution, or use of energy. Under the EO, SEE's must include an analysis of the adverse effects of the proposed rule and a discussion of alternatives. The EO also required agencies to submit their SEE's to OIRA.

e. Executive Order 13272

By Executive Order 13272, 67 Fed. Reg. 53461 (2002), President George W. Bush required agencies to establish procedures designed to ensure compliance with the Regulatory Flexibility Act.

f. Executive Order 13563

In January, 2011 President Barack Obama issued a new Executive Order on regulatory review, 76 Fed. Reg. 3821 (2011) stressing public participation in rulemaking (including via the Internet), posting of rulemaking dockets on regulations.gov, and periodic agency review of existing rules, to make each agency's regulatory program more efficient and less burdensome.

H. STATE RULEMAKING PROCEDURES

Most states tend to use informal, notice-and-comment, rulemaking processes. *See* A. Bonfield, State Administrative Rule Making (Little, Brown and Co., 1986). However, some states have imposed hybrid requirements. *See generally* Marsha N. Cohen, *Regulatory Reform: Assessing the California Plan*, 1983 Duke L. J. 231.

I. NEGOTIATED RULEMAKING

In recent years, there has been a movement to implement so-called "negotiated rulemaking." *See* Negotiated Rulemaking Act, 5 U.S.C.A. §§ 561 *et seq.* The hope is that through negotiation, as opposed to adversarial relationships, the parties can "cooperatively agree on creative solutions to problems." Administrative

Conference of the United States, Recommendation 82–4, 1 CFR § 305.82–4. If they succeed, the negotiated rule is then formalized through an ordinary rulemaking process.

1. Notice of Intent

The Administrative Conference of the United States (ACUS) recommends that negotiated rulemaking begin with a notice in the *Federal Register* that indicates that an agency "is contemplating developing a rule by negotiation and indicates in the notice the issues involved and the participants and interests already identified." A.C.U.S., Recommendation 82–4, 1 CFR § 305.82–4.

2. The Results of Negotiated Rulemaking

ACUS recommends that the results of a negotiated rulemaking be published and formalized in the same way that other rules are published and formalized: "The agency should publish the negotiated text of the proposed rule in its notice of proposed rulemaking. If the agency does not publish the negotiated text as a proposed rule, it should explain its reasons. The agency may wish to propose amendments or modifications to the negotiated proposed rule, but it should do so in such a manner that the public at large can identify the work of the agency and of the negotiating group." A.C.U.S., Recommendation 82–4, 1 CFR § 305.82–4.

3. Review of Comments

ACUS contemplates that the negotiating group should be allowed to review comments on the proposed rule, and offer input about whether the negotiated rule should be modified. A.C.U.S., Recommendation 82–4, 1 CFR § 305.82–4. However, the agency should reserve for itself ultimate authority to decide whether to issue the rule.

J. JUDICIAL REVIEW OF RULES

When agencies create rules, courts are free to substantively review the results of those rules on the basis that the rule is inconsistent with the agency's governing statute, or that the rule is either arbitrary and capricious (in the case of informal rulemaking) or lacks substantial evidence (in the case of formal rulemaking).

1. Statutory Interpretation

Section 706 of the APA directs reviewing courts to hold unlawful agency action "not in accordance with law," 5 U.S.C.A. § 706(2)(A), and agency action "in excess of statutory jurisdiction, authority, or limitations, or short of statutory right," *id.* § 706(2)(C).

a. *Marbury* and Judicial Authority

In *Marbury v. Madison*, 5 U.S. (1 Cranch) 137, 2 L. Ed. 60 (1803), the United States Supreme Court stated that "It is emphatically the province and duty of the judicial department to say what the law is." As a result, the courts have the power to review most agency action, including the content of administrative rules and regulations. However, subject to constitutional limitations, Congress may make agency actions unreviewable by courts. *See* 5 U.S.C.A. § 701(a)(1). Other agency actions may be unreviewable if they are held to be "committed to agency discretion by law." *See id.* § 701(a)(2). *See generally* Chapter 4 for a discussion of the reviewability of agency action.

b. Deference to Administrative Action

Even though the federal courts have the power to review rules and regulations, courts are frequently deferential to administrative action. They are deferential for a variety of reasons. In creating administrative regulations, agencies act pursuant to congressionally delegated authority. Moreover, agencies frequently have expertise in their assigned areas, and therefore a greater understanding of regulatory issues than courts.

c. *Chevron* Deference

In *Chevron U.S.A., Inc. v. Natural Resources Defense Council, Inc.*, 467 U.S. 837, 104 S.Ct. 2778, 81 L.Ed.2d 694 (1984), the Court suggested that reviewing courts should be deferential to agency-issued rules interpreting its authorizing statute: "When a court reviews an agency's construction of the statute which it administers, it is confronted with two questions. First, always, is the question whether Congress has directly spoken to the precise question at issue. If the intent of Congress is clear, that is the end of the matter; for the court, as well as the agency, must give effect to the unambiguously expressed intent of Congress. If, however, the court determines Congress has not directly addressed the precise question at issue, the court does not simply impose its own construction on the statute, as would be necessary in the absence of an administrative interpretation. Rather, if the statute is silent or ambiguous with respect to the specific issue, the question for the court is whether the agency's answer is based on a permissible construction of the statute."

d. The Mechanics of *Chevron* Deference

In *Chevron*, the Court justified its deferential approach on the following grounds: " 'The power of an administrative agency to administer a congressionally created . . . program necessarily requires the formulation of policy and the making of rules to fill any gap left, implicitly or explicitly, by Congress.' If Congress has explicitly left a gap for the agency to fill, there is an express delegation of authority to the agency to elucidate a specific provision of the statute by regulation. Such legislative regulations are given controlling weight unless they are arbitrary, capricious, or manifestly contrary to the statute. Sometimes the legislative delegation to an agency on a particular question is implicit rather than explicit. In such a case, a court may not substitute its own construction of a statutory provision for a reasonable interpretation made by the administrator of an agency."

e. The Justifications for *Chevron* Deference

In *Chevron*, the Court articulated the following additional justifications for its approach to deference: "Judges are not experts in the field, and are not part of either political branch of the Government. Courts must, in some cases, reconcile competing political interests, but not on the basis of the judges' personal policy preferences. In contrast, an agency to which Congress has delegated policy-making responsibilities may, within the limits of that delegation, properly rely upon the incumbent administration's views of wise policy to inform its judgments. While agencies are not directly accountable to the people, the Chief Executive is, and it is entirely appropriate for this political branch of the Government to make such policy choices—resolving the competing interests which Congress itself either inadvertently did not resolve, or intentionally left to be resolved by the agency charged with the administration of the statute in light of everyday realities."

f. *Chevron* and Prior Inconsistent Judicial Rulings

If a court has previously interpreted a statutory provision, an agency may not act inconsistently with that interpretation unless that interpretation recognized room for agency discretion. *See National Cable & Telecommunications Ass'n v. Brand X Internet Service*, 545 U.S. 967, 982, 125 S.Ct. 2688, 2700, 162 L.Ed.2d 820 (2005) (a court's "prior judicial construction of a statute trumps an agency construction otherwise entitled to *Chevron* deference only if the prior court decision holds that its construction follows from the unambiguous terms of the statute and thus leaves no room for agency discretion."). However, if that interpretation did leave such room, then a subsequent agency interpretation should receive *Chevron* deference and be upheld if reasonable, despite the earlier judicial ruling.

g. *Chevron*'s Applicability

Chevron is not the only deference standard used by the Court to review agency statutory interpretations. In *U.S. v. Mead Corp.*, 533 U.S. 218, 121 S.Ct. 2164, 150 L.Ed.2d 292 (2001), the Court held that in some situations, in particular (but not only) when the agency uses an especially informal and decentralized interpretive process, *Chevron* should not apply. In such a case, the agency interpretation would receive deference based on the formula enunciated in *Skidmore v. Swift & Co.*, 323 U.S. 134, 65 S.Ct. 161, 89 L.Ed. 124 (1944). "*Skidmore* deference" accords deference to agency statutory interpretations to the extent the court is convinced by factors such as the cogency's of the agency's analysis and the care with which it answered the interpretive question.

2. Substantive Content of Rules

Section 706 provides that a "reviewing court shall . . . hold unlawful and set aside agency action, findings, and conclusions found to be—(A) arbitrary, capricious, an abuse of discretion, or not otherwise in accordance with law; . . . [and] (E) unsupported by substantial evidence in a case subject to sections 556 and 557 of this title [*i.e.*, in a case where the agency was required to follow formal rulemaking procedures]. . . . " 5 U.S.C.A. § 706.

a. Scope of Review

Section 706 applies the "substantial evidence" test when agencies must create rules using formal procedures (trial-type procedures) under APA sections 556–557. By contrast, when an agency proceeds by notice and comment, the APA mandates application of the "arbitrary and capricious" standard. However, in some cases, Congress imposes a different standard of review.

b. "Substantial Evidence" Defined

The "substantial evidence" standard focuses on whether the record contains "such evidence as a reasonable mind might accept as adequate to support a conclusion." *Consolidated Edison v. NLRB*, 305 U.S. 197, 229, 59 S.Ct. 206, 216, 83 L.Ed. 126 (1938). By applying a "reasonable mind" standard, this standard suggests that agencies have discretion to choose among "reasonable" choices and that a reviewing court should not substitute its preference for the agency's. The standard does not require that the court agree with the agency's conclusions; it only requires that the agency's choice is a reasonable one, even if the court would have made another choice.

c. Arbitrary and Capricious Standard

As the name suggests, the "arbitrary and capricious" standard requires courts to be deferential to agency action. *See, e.g., Pacific States Box & Basket Co. v. White*, 296 U.S. 176, 56 S.Ct. 159, 80 L.Ed. 138 (1935). However, in *Citizens to Preserve Overton Park v. Volpe*, 401 U.S. 402, 91 S.Ct. 814, 28 L.Ed.2d 136 (1971), the Court held that the arbitrary and capricious standard "require[s] the reviewing court to engage in a substantial inquiry. . . . a thorough, probing in-depth review. . . . To [find arbitrariness], the court must consider whether the decision was based on a consideration of relevant factors and whether there has been a clear error of judgment. . . . Although this inquiry into the facts is to be searching and careful, the ultimate standard of review is a narrow one." Many believe that, in practice, there is little difference between the "arbitrary and capricious" and "substantial evidence" standards.

d. Rulemaking Record

Section 706 requires that a court "review the whole record" when determining whether to affirm a rule. When trial-type procedures are used under sections 556–557, Section 706 contemplates review of the trial record. By contrast, when informal procedures are used, the record is less clear-cut. In *Overton Park*, the Court defined the record for informal rulemakings to include the information the agency actually considered in making the decision. At the very least, the record includes the NOPR(s), comments received in response to the NOPR, and the final rule. The record might also include any studies or data relied on by the agency in promulgating the rule.

e. "Unknowable Facts"

In *Baltimore Gas & Electric Co. v. Natural Resources Defense Council*, 462 U.S. 87, 103 S.Ct. 2246, 76 L.Ed.2d 437 (1983), the Court dealt with a Nuclear Regulatory Commission rule regarding the effect of nuclear waste storage on the environment. Because the risks associated with such storage were uncertain, the Court concluded that a reviewing court should be deferential to the agency's conclusions: "Resolution of these fundamental policy issues lies . . . with Congress and the agencies to which Congress has delegated authority."

f. Adequate Explanation

Some courts have applied the arbitrary and capricious standard by inquiring whether there are "adequate reasons" to support the agency's choices. *See Motor Vehicle Manufacturers Assoc. of U.S., Inc. v. State Farm*

Mutual Automobile Ins. Co., 463 U.S. 29, 103 S.Ct. 2856, 77 L.Ed.2d 443 (1983) ("the agency must examine the relevant data and articulate a satisfactory explanation for its action including a 'rational connection between the facts found and the choice made.' "). If no "adequate explanation" exists, the court should reverse and remand to the agency.

g. Agency Changes of View

One difficult question is whether courts should give closer scrutiny to an agency decision when it reverses course. In *FCC v. Fox Television Stations*, 556 U.S. 502, 129 S.Ct. 1800, 173 L.Ed.2d 738 (2009), a five-justice majority of the Court rejected the idea of closer judicial scrutiny in such situations. However, Justice Kennedy, who comprised part of that majority, expressed doubt about a general rule on this question: "The question whether a change in policy requires an agency to provide a more-reasoned explanation than when the original policy was first announced is not susceptible, in my view, to an answer that applies in all cases." *Id.* at 535.

TRUE–FALSE QUESTIONS

1. There are three methods by which agencies can create legislative rules (depending on their governing statute): formal procedures, informal procedures and hybrid procedures.

2. An agency must use formal procedures when its governing statute requires that rules be made "after hearing."

3. An informal rulemaking is commenced by the issuance of a Notice of Proposed Rulemaking (NOPR).

4. In the informal rulemaking process, although an agency must allow interested parties to submit comments on the NOPR, the agency is not required to actually consider those comments.

5. When an agency is required to use informal rulemaking procedures, courts can require the agency to supplement those procedures with some aspects of trial-type procedure (e.g., the opportunity to present witnesses and to cross-examine opposing witnesses).

6. Formal rulemaking procedures are considered preferable to informal procedures because they are regarded as "more thorough" and "more likely to produce a better outcome."

7. Because *Marbury v. Madison* makes it "emphatically the province and duty of the judiciary to say what the law is," courts should critically review rules that agencies promulgate.

8. Agencies may not engage in negotiated rulemakings because such procedures compromise their inherent regulatory authority.

9. Formal rules are evaluated under the "arbitrary and capricious" standard.

10. Informal rules are evaluated under the "arbitrary and capricious" standard.

MULTIPLE CHOICE QUESTIONS

1. The informal rulemaking process does not include which of the following procedures:

    A. The issuance of a NOPR;

    B. The right of interested parties to submit comments on the NOPR;

    C. The right of interested parties to make oral presentations regarding the NOPR;

    D. Consideration of the written comments submitted by interested parties.

2. When a court applies *Chevron* deference to an informal rule, a reviewing court should ask which of the following questions:

    A. Whether Congress has explicitly instructed the courts to apply *Chevron* deference;

    B. Whether the intent of Congress is clear;

    C. Whether the agency has opted for a discretionary process;

    D. Whether Congress has prohibited courts from exercising their *Marbury*-authorized authority to "say what the law is."

3. If, in applying *Chevron* deference to an agency's statutory interpretation, the Court concludes that Congress' intent regarding the meaning of the governing statute is unclear, a reviewing court should evaluate the agency's rulemaking decisions under the following standard:

    A. Whether the agency's choice is "reasonable";

B. Whether the agency's decision is supported by "substantial evidence";

C. Whether the agency's decision is "arbitrary and capricious";

D. Whether the agency has provided an "adequate explanation."

ESSAY QUESTIONS

1. Under *Marbury v. Madison*, it is "emphatically the province and duty of courts to say what the law is." If so, why do courts apply *Chevron* deference when they review an agency's legislative rules?

2. Describe the purpose and function of the informal rulemaking process.

3. Explain why reviewing courts are not allowed to impose agency procedural requirements, beyond notice and comment requirements, in informal rulemaking procedures under the APA.

ANSWERS TO TRUE–FALSE QUESTIONS

1. True. There are in fact three methods by which agencies can create legislative rules (depending on their governing statute): formal procedures and informal procedures (both set forth in the APA), and hybrid procedures.

2. False. Formal rulemaking procedures are not invoked by a requirement that rules be made "after hearing." Formal procedures are required when APA sections 556 & 557 are specifically invoked by use of the specific terms "on the record after opportunity for agency hearing," as well as when the governing statute explicitly indicates that formal procedures are invoked.

3. True. An informal rulemaking is commenced by the issuance of a Notice of Proposed Rulemaking (NOPR).

4. False. The APA has been interpreted by court to require agencies to actually consider the comments, as part of the agency's obligation to receive comments.

5. False. In *Vermont Yankee*, the Court held that, when an agency is required by statute to use only informal rulemaking procedures, courts

cannot require the agency to supplement those procedures with some aspects of trial-type procedure (e.g., the opportunity to present witnesses and to cross-examine opposing witnesses).

6. False. As a general rule, formal rulemaking procedures are considered less preferable because they are difficult and time-consuming to use, and because they are generally not well suited to the process by which broad policy decisions are best made. As a result, when agencies are forced to use formal procedures, they rarely choose to articulate policy legislatively.

7. False. Even though *Marbury v. Madison* makes it "emphatically the province and duty of the judiciary to say what the law is," courts are frequently deferential in reviewing rules that agencies promulgate.

8. False. Congress has encouraged agencies to engage in negotiated rulemakings in the hope that rules can be produced by consensus.

9. False. Under APA Section 706 formal rules are evaluated under the "substantial evidence" standard.

10. True. Under APA Section 706 informal rules are evaluated under the "arbitrary and capricious" standard.

ANSWERS TO MULTIPLE CHOICE QUESTIONS

1. Answer (C) is correct. The informal rulemaking process includes Answer (A) (the issuance of a NOPR), Answer (B) (the right of interested parties to submit comments on the NOPR), and Answer (D) (consideration of the written comments submitted by interested parties). Informal procedures do not include Answer (C) (the right of interested parties to make oral presentations regarding the NOPR).

2. Answer (B) is correct. In deciding whether to apply *Chevron* deference to an informal rule, a reviewing court should ask whether the intent of Congress is clear. If it is clear, both the courts and the agencies are bound by it. Answer (A) is incorrect because Congress rarely if ever explicitly instructs courts to apply Chevron deference. Answer (C) is incorrect because courts do not focus on whether an agency has opted for a discretionary process. Answer (D) is incorrect because courts do not ask whether Congress has prohibited courts from exercising their *Marbury*-authorized authority to "say what the law is."

3. Answer (A) is correct. If, in applying *Chevron* deference to an agency's statutory interpretation, the Court concludes that Congress' intent regarding the meaning of the governing statute is unclear, a reviewing court should evaluate the agency's rulemaking decisions by asking whether the agency's choice is "reasonable." Answer (B) is incorrect because courts do not ask whether the agency's decision is supported by "substantial evidence." Answer (C) is incorrect because courts do not ask whether the agency's decision is "arbitrary and capricious." Answer (D) is incorrect because courts do not ask whether the agency has provided an "adequate explanation."

ANSWERS TO ESSAY QUESTIONS

1. In *Chevron U.S.A., Inc. v. Natural Resources Defense Council, Inc.*, 467 U.S. 837, 104 S.Ct. 2778, 81 L.Ed.2d 694 (1984), the Court offered the following justifications for being deferential to agency decisionmaking when the intent of Congress is unclear. These justifications point to the agency's superior legitimacy in setting regulatory policy, as compared with courts:

    > Judges are not experts in the field, and are not part of either political branch of the Government. Courts must, in some cases, reconcile competing political interests, but not on the basis of the judges' personal policy preferences. In contrast, an agency to which Congress has delegated policy-making responsibilities may, within the limits of that delegation, properly rely upon the incumbent administration's views of wise policy to inform its judgments. While agencies are not directly accountable to the people, the Chief Executive is, and it is entirely appropriate for this political branch of the Government to make such policy choices—resolving the competing interests which Congress itself either inadvertently did not resolve, or intentionally left to be resolved by the agency charged with the administration of the statute in light of everyday realities.

    > When a challenge to an agency construction of a statutory provision, fairly conceptualized, really centers on the wisdom of the agency's policy, rather than whether it is a reasonable choice within a gap left open by Congress, the challenge must fail. In such a case, federal judges—who have no constituency—have a duty to respect legitimate policy choices made by those who do. The responsibilities for assessing the wisdom of such policy choices and resolving the struggle between competing views of the public interest are not judicial ones: "Our Constitution vests such responsibilities in the political branches."

2. The informal rulemaking process is designed to give interested parties the chance to comment on proposed agency action. The hope is that, by receiving and considering those comments, agencies will make better decisions, with an appropriate amount of public input through an informal process that best reflects the nature of rulemaking. The process proceeds by requiring agencies to publish a NOPR in the *Federal Register*, allowing interested parties to submit comments on the NOPR, and requiring the agencies to consider the comments in issuing its final rule.

3. In *Vermont Yankee*, the Court concluded that APA procedures involve a compromise between giving parties procedural rights and allowing the agency the flexibility to regulate effectively and efficiently. In other words, some interests wanted to subject administrative agencies to greater procedures while others wanted to subject them to fewer procedures. Congress compromised by adopting the APA's notice and comment process. Given this compromise, it would be inappropriate to allow the courts to upset this delicate balance by imposing procedures of their own design. Note, though, that if it wishes, Congress can always mandate additional procedures in the statute authorizing the agency to act.

CHAPTER TWO

Adjudications

A. INTRODUCTION

Adjudications and regulations are the two fundamental methods by which agencies impose legal obligations on private parties.

1. Adjudications Result in Orders

The APA defines adjudication as the "agency process for the formulation of an order." In turn, an order is defined as "the whole or part of any final disposition . . . in a matter other than rule making."

2. Rules Are Distinguished by Their Prospective Effect

A rule is defined as "the whole or a part of an agency statement of general or particular applicability and future effect designed to implement, interpret or prescribe law or policy . . . " Thus, adjudications are the process by which any final disposition other than one of future effect is reached.

3. The Rule/Order Distinction Tracks the Legislative/Judicial Distinction

In general, agency adjudications can be thought of as proceedings in which law is applied retrospectively to a party, just as in a normal court proceeding.

B. INFORMAL ADJUDICATION: INTRODUCTION

1. The Trigger for Formal Adjudication Is a Procedure Required to Be "On the Record After Opportunity for an Agency Hearing"

As described in the next section, the APA prescribes procedures for adjudications "required by statute to be determined on the record after opportunity for an agency hearing." 5 U.S.C. § 554(a). The same language is used to distinguish when agencies must engage in formal, as opposed to informal, rulemaking.

2. Courts Sometimes Do not Require Strict Adherence to This Language When Considering Whether Adjudications Have to Follow the APA's Formal Procedures

However, while courts in the rulemaking context have held that agencies need only satisfy the informal rulemaking procedures unless Congress has used those exact words, courts have been more willing to read less than these precise words as requiring formal adjudication procedures. The logic is that there should be a presumption of informality in rulemaking, since the rulemaking process is not conducive to formal, trial-type procedures. By contrast, courts are more willing to insist on formality in adjudication, since adjudication in general is thought of as a relatively formalized process.

3. The APA Requires No Particular Procedure for Informal Adjudications

When a court interprets the authorizing statute to not require formal adjudicatory procedures, the APA provides no guide as to what constitutes acceptable informal adjudication procedure.

4. In Cases of Informal Adjudication, the Due Process Clause Sets the Required Procedures

The APA's lack of procedures for informal adjudications does not mean that in such situations agencies are completely free to use whatever procedures they wish (or none at all). Instead, if the Due Process clause of the Constitution applies, then it may mandate particular procedures.

C. WHEN THE DUE PROCESS CLAUSE IS TRIGGERED

1. Applicability of the Due Process Clause

The Due Process clause is generally thought to apply only to adjudications.

2. Due Process Triggered Only by Particularized Actions

In cases from the early 20th century, the Supreme Court distinguished situations where government action affected a large number of parties on grounds common to all of them, holding that in such situations government did not need to provide a hearing. By contrast, when a small number of persons were affected, each on grounds particular to them, Due Process would apply. *Londoner v. Denver*, 210 U.S. 373, 28 S.Ct. 708, 52 L.Ed. 1103 (1908); *Bi–Metallic Inv. Co. v. State Bd. of Equalization*, 239 U.S. 441, 36 S.Ct. 141, 60 L.Ed. 372 (1915).

D. DUE PROCESS REQUIRES THREE INQUIRIES

Assuming a particularized decision, the question then becomes the elements of Due Process doctrine. Modern Due Process requires the following steps:

- a determination that a life, liberty or property interest is at stake;

- a deprivation of that interest; and

- a determination of how much process is due before such a deprivation can take place

The next three sections treat each of these elements in order.

E. THE EXISTENCE OF A DUE PROCESS INTEREST

1. Historically the Court Recognized Relatively Few Due Process—Protected Interests

Historically, only interests protectable at common law were recognized as protected interests. Such interests would include property and contract rights, and personal rights such as freedom to move about.

2. Modern Due Process Law Protects a Larger Number of Interests

Starting in the late 1960's, the Court began to reconceptualize property and liberty to include not just common law-protected interests, but also interests that had been provided by statute, and upon which individuals could reasonably be expected to rely.

3. Modern Due Process Law Bases Its Analysis on Expectations

This new conception of property and liberty was based on the theory that the basic idea of property was grounded on individuals' reliance expectations, and that in the post-New Deal era individuals had come to expect not just on government protection of traditional property, but also on the continuation of benefits that earlier doctrine had described as mere gratuities.

4. Under Modern Doctrine Licenses and Other Government Benefits Constitute Property

Under the modern rule, regulatory benefits such as licenses to practice law and veterans' benefits are treated more like property.

5. Due Process Interests Can Still Be Destroyed by Government Acting Against the Entire Class

Under the modern analysis, the legislature could destroy an interest like a veteran's benefit, by repealing the statute granting those benefits. However, it the government kept the benefit scheme in place but decided that a particular individual did not qualify, then that person would have a due process interest. It was this analysis which led the Court in *Goldberg v. Kelly*, 397 U.S. 254, 90 S.Ct. 1011, 25 L.Ed.2d 287 (1970) to describe welfare benefits as due process-protected "property" and as interests that could not be taken away from an individual without due process.

6. **Liberty Interests Are Analyzed Similarly**

    This doctrine also encompasses liberty interests, with the result that any governmental commitment to provide liberty would be held to engender reasonable expectations on the part of the beneficiary, and thus would be protected by due process. Thus, even though a prison might not be constitutionally required to provide some relatively trivial liberty interest to a prisoner—say, a set amount of daily exercise time—if the government committed to providing that benefit, for example, by promising to do so in a prison manual, that interest might be protected by due process.

7. **Liberty Interests Can Also Be Found in the Due Process Clause's Liberty Prong Itself**

    In addition, more substantial liberty interests, *e.g.*, the right to marry, are protected independent of this analysis, by operation of the "liberty" component of the Due Process clause itself.

8. **The Expectations Approach to Liberty No Longer Applies in the Prison Context**

    The application of this expectation analysis to liberty interests came under strain in the prison context. It was generally accepted as good policy for prisons to cabin administrators' and guards' discretion by enacting rules. But the combination of prisons' adversarial environment and the Court's expectations analysis encouraged prisoners to bring a great many procedural due process claims based on deprivations of trivial liberty interests that had been promised somewhere in a regulation.

9. **In Prison Contexts the Liberty Interest Must Be Significant in Itself in Order for Due Process to Apply**

    In *Sandin v. Conner*, 515 U.S. 472, 115 S.Ct. 2293, 132 L.Ed.2d 418 (1995), the Court stated that only "atypical and significant" deprivations beyond the confinement itself would count as due process protected interests.

F. DEPRIVATIONS MUST BE DELIBERATE

While "deprivation" might seem to connote any impairment at issue, the Supreme Court has ruled that a person is "deprived" of a due process protected interest only when the government has deliberately impaired that interest. *Daniels v. Williams*, 474 U.S. 327, 106 S.Ct. 662, 88 L.Ed.2d 662 (1986). Accidental government deprivations might give rise to a tort suit, but they do not implicate due process *per se*.

G. THE PROCESS THAT IS "DUE" IS BASED ON A BALANCING TEST

1. Expansion of the Interests Protected by Due Process Has Been Accompanied by a Reduction of the Process That Is Due

Assuming that government has deprived an individual of a due process protected interest, the question then arises whether the government has provided sufficient, or "due," process. In recent decades, as the Court has expanded the number of interests protected by due process, it has also reduced the amount of process that the Constitution requires.

2. The Court Employs a Balancing Test to Determine What Process Is Due

In *Mathews v. Eldridge*, 424 U.S. 319, 96 S.Ct. 893, 47 L.Ed.2d 18 (1976), the Court set forth a three part balancing test to determine how much process is due. The test requires a court to balance (1) the importance of the interest to the class of recipients; (2) the chance of erroneous deprivations under the current procedures and the increased accuracy the requested procedures would produce; and (3) the government's interest.

3. As Applied in *Mathews* Disability Benefits Were Not as Important as the Welfare Benefits in *Goldberg v. Kelly*

In *Mathews*, which dealt with a cut-off of social security disability benefits, with a hearing provided only after the benefits had been stopped, the Court noted that the benefits were not as important to the recipients as were the welfare payments in *Goldberg*, since welfare payments were predicated on a finding of need, unlike the disability payments.

4. The Nature of the Decision in *Mathews* Did Not Require an Oral Hearing to Improve Its Accuracy

With regard to the second factor, the *Mathews* Court noted that before the benefits cut off the beneficiary was afforded a chance to submit written evidence documenting his disability. The Court concluded that, since the issue to be decided was the beneficiary's medical condition, written evidence would be highly probative and the oral hearing requested by the plaintiff would not have led to more accurate decision making.

5. The Government's Interest in *Mathews* Was Not Trivial

Finally, the Court noted that the government had an interest in reducing both the administrative costs of oral hearings, and the costs of benefits paid during the pendency of hearings. On the latter point, the Court noted that while the government could try to recoup benefits inappropriately paid out, in reality it might be difficult to do so, given that many beneficiaries would have spent the benefits in the meantime and wouldn't be able to repay them.

6. *Mathews* Has Been Used to Justify a Hearing to Allow a Decision Maker to Make Better Use of His Discretion

Still, the *Mathews* factors are often not perfectly applicable to a given fact pattern. In some cases courts have expanded the concept of accurate decision making to include wise uses of discretion, thus requiring an oral hearing, even when technically the issue is completely resolvable based on written evidence.

7. Some Courts Have Gone Beyond *Mathews* to Give Effect to Other Concerns Underlying Due Process

Sometimes lower courts have gone completely beyond *Mathews*, to try to give effect to other due process values, such as the individual's dignitary interest in having an oral communication with a government decision maker, regardless of the *Mathews* calculus.

8. *Mathews* Creates a Flexible Test

In sum, while *Mathews* provides the general rule for determining the amount of process due, the factors are sufficiently vague that courts retain a great deal of leeway to judge cases according to their own sense of efficiency and equity.

9. Due Process Also Requires an Impartial Decision Maker

Beyond *Mathews*, due process requires an impartial decision maker. Usually impartiality is decided based on the particular facts of the situation.

10. Pecuniary Interests Constitute a *Per Se* Due Process Violation

One situation where impartiality is *per se* questioned is when the decision maker has a pecuniary interest in the outcome of the issue. For example due process would be violated if the decision maker is a sheriff whose salary is funded by the fines he adjudicates.

11. Personal Animus Is Also a *Per Se* Due Process Violation

Due process is also violated where the decision maker has a personal animus against the party.

12. Prejudgment of Adjudicative Facts Is Also Often a Due Process Violation

Prejudgment of an issue can be a problem if it is thought that the adjudicator has prejudged adjudicative facts about the party's claim; however, prejudgment about the law or more legislative-type facts is generally considered less of a problem. Indeed, federal judges often have strong preexisting beliefs about these latter issues, and yet they may continue to adjudicate claims that implicate them.

H. FORMAL ADJUDICATION

1. The APA Calls for Trial–Type Procedures in Formal Adjudication

The APA has detailed procedures for formal adjudicative processes. In general, these procedures, set forth at 5 U.S.C. §§ 554, 556 and 557, provide for the types of procedures normally found in trial courts.

2. Trial–Type Procedures Call for Oral Hearings, Cross–Examination and Decisions on the Record

Thus, parties have the right to request an oral hearing, to call witnesses and cross-examine the other side's witnesses, and to have a decision made on the record.

3. The ALJ Can Either Make the Decision or Recommend the Decision to Be Made by the Agency Head

The APA authorizes administrative law judges (ALJs) to reach a decision for the agency, or simply to recommend a decision to the agency head, who then makes the decision. Even if the ALJ makes the actual decision, agencies may if they wish provide for an appeal procedure to the agency head.

4. The APA Restricts *Ex Parte* Communications With Agency Personnel

Ex parte communications between administrative judges (ALJs) and others are the subject of two separate APA provisions. Section 554(d) of the APA provides explicit rules governing the *ex parte* communications of ALJs and agency heads conducting formal adjudications.

5. The Internal *Ex Parte* Communication Ban Applies to ALJs

That provision prohibits ALJs from speaking to any person about a fact in issue in the case, except on notice and opportunity to participate to the other side, and prohibits ALJs from being supervised by agency employees performing investigative or prosecutorial functions.

6. Agency Heads May Speak With Agency Personnel

Agency heads, who sometimes hear cases on appeal from ALJs, are exempt from these rules; however, witnesses and prosecutors are still limited to participating only in their respective capacities.

7. The APA Also Restricts *Ex Parte* Communications With Private Parties

Section 557(d) deals with *ex parte* communications between agency adjudicators (ALJs or agency heads) and persons outside the agency. It prohibits any such communication "relative to the merits of the proceeding."

8. The External *Ex Parte* Communications Ban Extends to the Adjudicator and to the Private Party

Note that the prohibition extends to communications initiated by both the adjudicator and the private party.

9. If *Ex Parte* Communications With a Private Party Occur the Adjudicator Must Memorialize and Disclose Them

If such a communication does occur, the adjudicator must describe its substance in a memorandum that is placed in the adjudicatory record, and provide an opportunity for parties to respond.

10. Knowing *Ex Parte* Communications Can Lead to a Ruling Against the Violating Party

If such a communication is knowingly made by a party—that is, made with knowledge that it is an *ex parte* communication—the adjudicator has the authority, but is not required, to punish it by ruling against that party on the merits.

TRUE–FALSE QUESTIONS

1. When performing a formal adjudication, the head of agency may consult an internal agency expert on a fact in issue in the case, if the expert did not testify in the case.

2. Procedural due process protects only those interests which the common law historically would protect by providing a cause of action in case of its deprivation.

3. The modern test for procedural due process simply balances the importance of the government interest in avoiding more process with the private party's interest in the underlying benefit.

4. The APA sets forth the procedural requirements for both informal and formal adjudications.

5. Under the APA agency heads may never make the initial decision in an agency adjudication.

6. For purposes of the Due Process clause, government does not "deprive" anyone of life, liberty or property if the deprivation results from an accident.

7. *Ex parte* communications made by an external party to an adjudicator, if made knowingly, can be punished by the adjudicator ruling against that party.

8. The determination of liberty interests in the context of prisoners' rights is treated differently than in other factual contexts.

MULTIPLE CHOICE QUESTION

Sam Louis is a veteran of the first Gulf War, where he was injured. As such since 1991 he has been collecting disability benefits from the Veterans Administration. Last month he received a letter informing him that his next check would be his last, as a review of his medical records indicated that he was no longer disabled. Which of the following statements, if true, would be the strongest support for Sam's claim that he had been deprived of a property interest protected by the Due Process Clause?

    A. Sam needs the benefits to live, as he is poor.

    B. As a class, disabled veterans generally depend on their disability benefits for life's necessities.

    C. The Veterans' Administration regulations, which Sam has never read, provide that disabled veterans are entitled to disability benefits.

    D. An oral hearing would be highly probative in proving to the administrator that Sam was in fact disabled.

ESSAY QUESTION

Assume that the Clean Air Act requires that adjudications of violations of the statute be performed "on the record after opportunity for agency hearing." The ALJ, in the course of the adjudication, makes a private phone call to an expert in the agency who did not testify in the case, asking him about some technical issues relevant to the case. While attending a dinner party, the ALJ is approached by the attorney for the party in the case, who proceeds to explain and expand upon a legal argument she made in her brief to the ALJ. Finally, correctly citing the agency's internal rules, the ALJ refuses to reach a final decision on the matter, but instead files with the head of the agency proposed fact findings and legal conclusions and a recommended result for the agency head's consideration. What issues are implicated by this set of facts?

ANSWERS TO TRUE–FALSE QUESTIONS

1. True. 5 U.S.C. § 554(d) disables an ALJ from consulting in that way, but it allows an agency head to do so.

2. False. Today, except in the prison context, due process property and liberty interests may also be determined by reference to whether government conduct created a reasonable expectation as to the continuation of that interest.

3. False. An important part of the modern test for what process is due concerns the accuracy of the decisions made under the current procedure, and the increased accuracy that might flow from the procedures requested by the plaintiff.

4. False. The APA does not set forth procedures for informal adjudications.

5. False. The APA provides for ALJs to make the initial decision, or for ALJs simply to recommend a decision to the agency head.

6. True. Only intentional deprivations count as "deprivations" under the Due Process Clause.

7. True. 5 U.S.C. § 557(d) allows adjudicators to exercise this severe penalty.

8. True. After *Sandin v. Connor* prisoners' Due Process claims are not evaluated according to the reasonable expectation-analysis that governs these due process claims in other contexts.

ANSWER TO MULTIPLE CHOICE QUESTION

The correct answer is (C). which applies the expectation analysis currently used in procedural due process cases outside the prison context. (A) and (B) are incorrect because they go to the question of the importance of the benefit either to the individual claimant or to the class of claimants. Importance of the benefit to the class of claimant is relevant only to the question of how much process is due, not the question of whether there is a due process interest at stake in this case. The same thing can be said about (D), which applies the second *Mathews v. Eldridge* element for determining how much process is due.

ANSWER TO ESSAY QUESTION

The adjudication must be conducted pursuant to the formal adjudication requirements of the APA, given that the language of the authorizing statute tracks precisely the APA's triggering language for formal adjudication. Under those procedures, the ALJ violated § 554(d) by making the *ex parte* communication to the expert. The party's attorney violated § 557(d) by making the *ex parte* communication at the dinner party, and the ALJ should have cured it by memorializing the substance of the communication and allowing other parties to respond. However, there is no APA violation in the agency's regulations making the agency head the decision maker of first resort; the APA allows both that practice and the ALJ making the first decision in the case.

CHAPTER THREE

Choice of Procedures and Non–Legislative Rules

A. NON–LEGISLATIVE RULES DEFINED

The term "non-legislative rule" extends to a variety of administrative pronouncements such as adjudicative rules, policy statements and interpretive rules. Even though such rules are not necessarily binding, they do constitute "rules" because they fit the APA's definition of a "rule"—"the whole or a part of an agency statement of general or particular applicability and future effect designed to implement, interpret, or prescribe law or policy. . . . " 5 U.S.C.A. § 551(4).

B. DISTINGUISHED FROM LEGISLATIVE RULES

Non-legislative rules can be distinguished from "legislative rules" by virtue of the way they are created. Legislative rules are promulgated using the APA's rulemaking procedures, and are legally binding. 5 U.S.C.A. § 553. As we shall see, "non-legislative rules" can be created using a variety of procedures.

C. TYPES OF NON–LEGISLATIVE RULES

Under Section 553 of the Administrative Procedure Act, there are two different types of non-legislative rules: "interpretative rules" and "general statements of policy." Both are exempt from APA Section 553's rulemaking procedures. However, "adjudicative rules," "rules" announced by agencies in adjudicative proceedings, also qualify as non-legislative rules.

1. Preference for Legislative Rules

In general, legislative procedures are considered to be a fairer, and more appropriate, method for making rules. There are two reasons. First, since legislative rules generally have prospective effect, whereas adjudicative rules are frequently applied retroactively, legislative rules provide regulated entities with greater notice regarding regulatory requirements and an opportunity to bring their conduct into compliance. Second, since legislative procedures are subject to rulemaking processes (meaning that the agency must announce the proposed rule and give interested parties the opportunity to comment and provide input), they ensure greater public participation and input into the rulemaking process.

2. Choice of Adjudication Over Rulemaking

In *Securities and Exchange Commission v. Chenery Corporation*, 332 U.S. 194, 67 S.Ct. 1575, 91 L.Ed. 1995 (1947), even though the United States Supreme Court expressed a preference for legislative procedures over adjudicative procedures, the Court held that administrative agencies have discretion about whether to articulate new rules legislatively or adjudicatively. In other words, they can articulate new "rules" and "policies" in adjudicative proceedings.

3. Need for Adjudicative Rules

Chenery II went on to note that "[not] every principle essential to the effective administration of a statute can or should be cast immediately into the mold of a general rule. Some principles must await their own development, while others must be adjusted to meet particular, unforeseeable situations. In performing its important functions in these respects, therefore, an administrative agency must be equipped to act either by general rule or by individual order. To insist upon one form of action to the exclusion of the other is to exalt form over necessity."

4. Impossibility of Creating All Rules Legislatively

In *Chenery II*, the Court went on to suggest that it would be difficult for administrative agencies to articulate all policies legislatively: "problems may arise in a case which the administrative agency could not reasonably foresee, problems which must be solved despite the absence of a relevant general rule. Or the agency may not have had sufficient experience with a particular problem to warrant rigidifying its tentative judgment into a hard and fast rule. Or the problem may be so specialized and varying in nature as to be impossible of capture within the boundaries of a general rule. In those situations, the agency must retain power to deal with the problems on a case-to-case basis if the administrative process is to be effective. There is thus a very definite place for the case-by-case evolution of statutory standards. And the choice made between proceeding by general rule or by individual, ad hoc litigation is one that lies primarily in the informed discretion of the administrative agency."

5. Adjudicative Rules May Be Valid Even if Retroactively Applied

Chenery II also recognized that adjudicative rules may cause unfairness if they are retroactively applied, but the Court held that the mere presence of retroactivity is "not necessarily fatal to its validity. Every case of first impression has a retroactive effect, whether the new principle is announced by a court or by an administrative agency. But such retroactivity must be balanced against the mischief of producing a result which is contrary to a statutory design or to legal and equitable principles. If that mischief is greater than the ill effect of the retroactive application of a new standard, it is not the type of retroactivity which is condemned by law."

6. *Chenery II* Affirmed

Chenery II's holding has been reaffirmed in later cases, including *National Labor Relations Board v. Bell Aerospace Company Division of Textron, Inc.*, 416 U.S. 267, 94 S.Ct. 1757, 40 L.Ed.2d 134 (1974), and *NLRB v. Wyman–Gordon Co.*, 394 U.S. 759, 89 S.Ct. 1426, 22 L.Ed.2d 709 (1969).

7. Agency Preference for Adjudicative Procedures

Many administrative agencies prefer to use adjudicative processes to create rules because those processes are not as public. When an agency announces a legislative procedure, there is the possibility that various interest groups (e.g., interested national organizations, companies and others) will campaign for or against the rule. By contrast, adjudicative processes are likely to attract less attention because they are less public. In addition, adjudicative processes are frequently easier and less expensive than national rulemaking proceedings. Finally, adjudicative processes are not subject to many of the procedural requirements applicable to legislative proceedings (e.g., cost-benefit analyses, OMB review, and congressional reviews).

8. *Wyman–Gordon* and the Excelsior Rule

In *National Labor Relations Board v. Wyman–Gordon Co.*, 394 U.S. 759, 89 S.Ct. 1426, 22 L.Ed.2d 709 (1969), the United States Supreme Court dealt with the so-called *Excelsior Underwear* rule. That rule was articulated in an NLRB case, *Excelsior Underwear*, and involved an attempt by the NLRB create an adjudicative rule using quasi-legislative procedures. Although the "rule" was created in an adjudicative proceeding, the NLRB contacted certain interested parties and invited them to submit comments on the proposed rule. The NLRB suggested that its new "rule" would be applied only prospectively.

a.   Judicial Criticism of the *Excelsior Underwear* Procedure

In *Wyman–Gordon*, the Court criticized the NLRB's approach, and suggested that legislative procedures constitute a preferable method for articulating new rules.

b.   *Excelsior Underwear* Did Not Create a Valid Legislative Rule

In addition, the Court held that the *Excelsior Underwear* rule did not create a valid legislative rule. There had been no compliance with legislative procedures since a NOPR had not been published in the *Federal Register* and the NLRB had not invited all interested parties to submit comments.

c.   *Excelsior Underwear* Did Not Create a Valid Adjudicative Rule

In addition, the Court concluded that the NLRB had not created a valid adjudicative rule since the rule was not applied in the *Excelsior Underwear* case. As a result, the rule was simply dicta.

d.   Wyman–Gordon Was Forced to Comply With the Gist of the *Excelsior Underwear* Rule

Nonetheless, the Court ordered Wyman–Gordon to comply because the rule was validly imposed in the *Wyman–Gordon* case itself, and the rule constituted a valid adjudicative rule in that context.

D.   OTHER NON–LEGISLATIVE RULES (POLICY STATEMENTS AND INTERPRETIVE STATEMENTS)

Section 553 of the APA recognizes two types of non-legislative rules: interpretive rules and statements of policy. An interpretive rule is a statement "issued by an agency to advise the public of the agency's construction of the statutes and rules which it administers." Attorney General's Manual on the Administrative Procedure Act 30 n. 3 (1947). A policy statement is a statement "issued by an agency to advise the public prospectively of the manner in which the agency proposes to exercise a discretionary power." *Id.* The distinction between these two types of non-legislative rules will be considered in greater detail below. For now, it is sufficient to know that these rules warn the public of an agency interpretation of a statute or regulation, or reflect the agency's views on policy issues.

1. Justifications for Using Non–Legislative Rules

Just as adjudicative rules have a place in the administrative system, other non-legislative rules have a place as well. As *Chenery II* held, it is virtually impossible for agencies to articulate all policies legislatively. As a result, non-legislative rules serve a valid informational function by advising regulated entities about the agency's views regarding the meaning of a statute or regulation, and the agency's enforcement policy. With that guidance, regulated entities have fair notice of regulatory meaning and an opportunity to bring their conduct into compliance. In addition, non-legislative rules provide guidance to agency personnel who must interpret and apply the provisions.

2. Concerns Regarding Non–Legislative Rules

When agencies issue non-legislative rules that interpret statutory or regulatory provisions, they can place regulated entities in a difficult situation. Even if a regulated entity believes that an agency's interpretation of a statute or regulation is incorrect or unfair, the regulated entity may feel pressure to comply with the agency's interpretation. Otherwise, it risks the possibility of an enforcement action with possible fines and penalties. Of course, in such a situation, the regulated entity can challenge the agency's interpretation, but such challenges can be time-consuming and expensive. As a result, many regulated entities simply opt to comply with the agency's interpretation.

3. Publication Requirements

Even though the APA exempts policy statements from rulemaking procedures, it does require agencies to publish in the *Federal Register* "statements of general policy or interpretations of general applicability formulated and adopted by the agency." *Id*. § 552(a)(1)(D). In theory, the APA also imposes sanctions for noncompliance: "[A] person may not in any manner be required to resort to, or be adversely affected by, a matter required to be published in the *Federal Register* and not so published," except if the person "has actual and timely notice of the terms" of the matter. *Id*. § 552. However, courts rarely sanction agencies for failure to publish their interpretations and policy statements. *See* James T. O'Reilly, Federal Information Disclosure, § 6.05 at 6–19 (2d ed. 1995).

4. Disguised Legislative Rules

Some regulated entities challenge policy statements on the basis that they are really legislative rules and therefore should be subject to rulemaking procedures. Some courts agree, holding that some policy statements constitute legislative rules when they impose a new "duty" with "binding effect." For example, in *American Hospital Association v. Bowen*, 834 F.2d 1037 (D.C.Cir.1987), the court focused on whether a policy statement imposed new "rights and obligations" as the criterion for requiring legislative procedures.

5.   Difficulty of Characterization

Even though an interpretive rule or policy statement does not literally impose new "duties" or "rights and obligations," it is important to realize that many interpretive rules and policy statements can be treated like rules imposing new "rights" and "duties." As previously noted, regulated entities are reluctant to ignore agency statements of interpretations or policy for fear of prosecution. Therefore, although some commentators suggest that regulated entities are "free to ignore" interpretive statements, the reality is that regulated entities do so at their peril. In addition, since courts frequently "defer" to administrative interpretations, it can be quite risky to ignore an agency interpretation.

E.   DEFERENCE TO ADJUDICATIVE AND NON–LEGISLATIVE RULES

Moreover, even though the courts have the authority to independently interpret statutory and regulatory provisions, courts frequently defer to agency interpretations of those provisions. Courts often defer even though an agency has stated its interpretation in the form of an adjudicative rule or non-legislative rule.

1.   Scope of Deference

There has been some disagreement about what standard of deference should apply to agency interpretations, especially to non-legislative rules such as policy statements and administrative interpretations.

a.   *Skidmore* Deference

In some instances, courts apply so-called *Skidmore* deference in which they are not compelled to accept administrative interpretations, but instead treat them as a "a body of experience and informed judgment to which courts and litigants may properly resort for guidance." *Skidmore v. Swift & Co.*, 323 U.S. 134, 65 S.Ct. 161, 89 L.Ed. 124 (1944). "The weight of such a judgment in a particular case will depend upon the thoroughness evident in its consideration, the validity of its reasoning, its consistency with earlier and later pronouncements, and all those factors which give it power to persuade, if lacking power to control." *Id.*

b. ***Chevron* Deference**

Instead of *Skidmore* deference, courts sometimes apply an alternate deference standard referred to as *Chevron* deference. Under *Chevron* deference, if Congress' intent regarding the meaning of a provision is unclear, the courts should accept an agency's "reasonable" interpretation of that provision. *Chevron, U.S.A., Inc. v. Natural Resources Defense Council, Inc.*, 467 U.S. 837, 104 S.Ct. 2778, 81 L.Ed.2d 694 (1984).

c. Distinguishing *Chevron* Deference and *Skidmore* Deference

As the language suggests, *Chevron* deference is potentially more deferential to administrative action than *Skidmore* deference. Instead of requiring a reviewing court to independently determine the meaning of a regulatory provision, giving an agency interpretation the weight it is due after consideration of a variety of factors, *Chevron* requires a reviewing court to accept a "reasonable" interpretation of an ambiguous regulatory provision.

2. Application to Non–Legislative Rules

The Court has vacillated regarding whether *Chevron* deference or *Skidmore* deference should be applied to non-legislative rules. *Chevron* itself involved application of the *Chevron* standard to a legislative rule. As a result, many commentators questioned whether *Chevron* deference should apply to non-legislative rules.

a. The *Christensen* Decision

The Court has applied *Skidmore* deference to some non-legislative rules. For example, in *Christensen v. Harris County*, 529 U.S. 576, 120 S.Ct. 1655, 146 L.Ed.2d 621 (2000), the Court was confronted by an agency's "opinion letter" construing the meaning of a federal statute. The Court refused to apply *Chevron* deference: "Interpretations such as those in opinion letters—like interpretations contained in policy statements, agency manuals, and enforcement guidelines, all of which lack the force of law—do not warrant *Chevron*-style deference." Instead, the Court applied *Skidmore* deference and rejected the interpretation.

b. The *Mead* Decision

In *United States v. Mead Corporation*, 533 U.S. 218, 121 S.Ct. 2164, 150 L.Ed.2d 292 (2001), the Court refused to apply *Chevron* deference to a "ruling letter." However, *Mead* suggested that the Court had applied *Chevron* deference to some interpretations articulated by less formal means than rulemaking.

c.   The *Barnhart* Decision

The Court further muddied the waters in its later decision in *Barnhart v. Walton*, 535 U.S. 212, 122 S.Ct. 1265, 152 L.Ed.2d 330 (2002). In that case, although the agency had articulated its interpretation in a legislative rule, the rule was of relatively recent duration and one party argued that it did not deserve deference because it was developed in response to the litigation. The Court concluded that *Chevron* deference should apply anyway because the interpretation was of long standing, albeit articulated in less formal ways: "[T]he Agency's interpretation is one of long standing. And the fact that the Agency previously reached its interpretation through means less formal than "notice and comment" rulemaking does not automatically deprive that interpretation of the judicial deference otherwise its due. If this Court's opinion in *Christensen v. Harris County* suggested an absolute rule to the contrary, our later opinion in *United States v. Mead Corp.* denied the suggestion. Indeed, *Mead* pointed to instances in which the Court has applied *Chevron* deference to agency interpretations that did not emerge out of noticeand-comment rulemaking. It indicated that whether a court should give such deference depends in significant part upon the interpretive method used and the nature of the question at issue."

3.   Deference to an Agency's Interpretation of Its Own Regulations

In general, the Court has been strongly inclined to defer to an agency's interpretation of its own regulations.

a.   The Holding in *Bowles v. Seminole Rock*

In its landmark decision, *Bowles v. Seminole Rock & Sand Co.*, 325 U.S. 410, 65 S.Ct. 1215, 89 L.Ed. 1700 (1945), the Court concluded that: "The intention of Congress or the principles of the Constitution in some situations may be relevant in the first instance in choosing between various constructions. But the ultimate criterion is the administrative interpretation, which becomes of controlling weight unless it is plainly erroneous or inconsistent with the regulation."

b.   The Justifications for Deferring to an Agency's Interpretation of Its Own Regulation

Courts are more inclined to defer to an agency's interpretation of its own regulation because the agency was the promulgator of the regulation and therefore is more likely to be cognizant of the regulation's intended meaning and scope, as well as of the agency's own original intent. In addition, the agency is acting in a sphere of delegated authority.

F. RETROACTIVITY

In general, retroactivity is disfavored in the law. As a simple matter of fairness, if not due process, regulated entities are entitled to fair notice of the standards with which they must comply, and an opportunity to bring their conduct into compliance with those standards. Because retroactively applied rules are announced after the fact, they have the potential to deprive regulated entities of fair notice.

1. Retroactive Regulations

Although most administrative regulations are issued with prospective effect, it is sometimes permissible for agencies to promulgate regulations with retroactive effect. In *Bowen v. Georgetown University Hospital*, 488 U.S. 204, 109 S.Ct. 468, 102 L.Ed.2d 493 (1988), the Court held that an agency may not give a regulation retroactive effect absent explicit congressional authorization: "Retroactivity is not favored. . . . Thus, congressional enactments and administrative rules will not be construed to have retroactive effect unless their language requires this result . . . in express terms. Even where some substantial justification for retroactive rulemaking is presented, courts should be reluctant to find such authority absent an express statutory grant." Finding no express authority, *Bowen* held that the regulation at issue in that case could not be applied retroactively.

2. Retroactive Interpretations

When an agency adopts a rule with prospective effect, retroactivity problems may still arise as the rule is interpreted and applied.

a. Vagueness and Ambiguity

It is not uncommon for regulatory provisions to suffer from vagueness or ambiguity. Indeed, the concept of deference itself, including *Chevron* deference, is premised on uncertainty regarding the meaning of regulatory provisions.

b. Retroactive Application of Agency Pronouncements

If a regulatory provision suffers from vagueness or ambiguity, that provision will ultimately need interpretation in the context of a regulatory adjudication or an agency-issued interpretation. In some instances, these interpretations are applied retroactively. Interpretations announced in adjudications are usually applied retroactively. Even when an agency announces an interpretation in a non-adjudicative context (e.g., in a press release), the agency might view the interpretation as a "necessary" or "inevitable" interpretation of the regulation and therefore may seek to apply it retroactively. In either context, the retroactive application may be unfair to a regulated entity who was unaware of the interpretation.

3. Interpretations and the Right to Notice

In *General Electric Company v. U.S. Environmental Protection Agency*, 53 F.3d 1324 (D.C.Cir.1995), although the Court accepted an agency's interpretation of its own regulation, the court refused to allow the agency to apply the interpretation retroactively. The court stated: "Due process requires that parties receive fair notice before being deprived of property. The due process clause thus 'prevents . . . deference from validating the application of a regulation that fails to give fair warning of the conduct it prohibits or requires.' In the absence of notice—for example, where the regulation is not sufficiently clear to warn a party about what is expected of it—an agency may not deprive a party of property by imposing civil or criminal liability."

4. Methods of Giving Notice

However, as *General Electric* also recognized, "in many cases the agency's pre-enforcement efforts to bring about compliance will provide adequate notice. As a result, even if an interpretation is retroactively applied, the regulated entity may not be able to claim lack of notice."

a. Direct Notice

Sometimes, agencies provide direct notice to regulated entities. If, for example, an agency informs a regulated party that it must seek a permit for a particular action, but the party begins acting without seeking a permit, the agency's pre-violation contact with the regulated party might be regarded as adequate notice. As a result, the court might be more inclined to impose liability for noncompliance if the agency's interpretation was permissible.

b. Indirect Notice

As *General Electric* held, even when the agency has not provided a regulated entity with direct notice of its interpretation, the regulated entity may be on constructive notice: "If, by reviewing the regulations and other public statements issued by the agency, a regulated party acting in good faith would be able to identify, with 'ascertainable certainty,' the standards with which the agency expects parties to conform, then the agency has fairly notified a petitioner of the agency's interpretation."

G. ESTOPPEL

For decades, the accepted wisdom was that the government may not be "estopped" in the same sense in which a private individual might be estopped.

For example, in *Federal Crop Ins. Corporation v. Merrill*, 332 U.S. 380, 68 S.Ct. 1, 92 L.Ed. 10 (1947), the Court applied estoppel when a government agent promised a farmer that government insurance covered his crops. Because the program did not cover individuals in the farmer's situation, the Court held that the farmer could not recover notwithstanding the agency's prior representations to the contrary. The Court expressed concern that federal law precluded recovery in that case, and that an agent's misstatement could not overcome the requirements of federal law.

1. Justifications for the General Rule

The prohibition against estopping the government reflects a judicial intent to protect the public purse. In many cases, either Congress or administrative regulations provide guidelines regarding the expenditure of public funds. As a result, if Congress has provided for money to be spent in a particular way, or under defined criteria, courts are reluctant to require agencies to spend money inconsistently with the law or the criteria based solely on the representations of subordinate governmental officials.

2. The *Richmond* Exception

In *Office of Personnel Management v. Richmond*, 496 U.S. 414, 110 S.Ct. 2465, 110 L.Ed.2d 387 (1990), the Court qualified *Merrill* by noting that "erroneous oral and written advice given by a Government employee to a benefits claimant may give rise to estoppel against the Government and so entitle the claimant to a monetary payment not otherwise permitted by law." However, relying on the Appropriations Clause of the Constitution, Art. I, § 9, cl. 7, the Court concluded that an estoppel claim could not force the government to pay out money prohibited by law.

3. Other Exceptions

In *United States v. Pennsylvania Industrial Chemical Corporation*, 411 U.S. 655, 93 S.Ct. 1804, 36 L.Ed.2d 567 (1973), the Court held that an individual, who had reasonably relied on statements made by a government agent, could not be criminally prosecuted when he acted consistently with that advice. Criminal sanctions are regarded as particularly onerous and fair notice is a prerequisite.

4. Inconsistent Application

Even though estoppel principles might not explicitly apply to the government, courts might apply a form of estoppel when an agency has taken inconsistent positions regarding the meaning of a statutory or regulatory provision. Courts have held that agency action is arbitrary and capricious if the agency acts inconsistently with past decisions without explaining the basis for the change. Also, to the extent that the agency is asking a court to defer to its new interpretation, courts may refuse deference because the agency has not been consistent. In *North Haven Board of Education v. Bell*, 456 U.S. 512, 102 S.Ct. 1912, 72 L.Ed.2d 299 (1982), for example, the Supreme Court rejected an administrative interpretation because the agency had changed its interpretation of a regulation several times, once during the course of the judicial proceedings. The Court concluded that there was no interpretation to which to defer.

5. More on Inconsistency

But the prohibition against inconsistent application is not absolute. In *Rust v. Sullivan*, 500 U.S. 173, 111 S.Ct. 1759, 114 L.Ed.2d 233 (1991), the Court held that consistency is not necessary to obtain deference, at least where the agency justifies the change with a reasoned analysis.

TRUE–FALSE QUESTIONS

1. Agencies may only articulate "rules" using notice and comment procedures.

2. The definition of a "non-legislative" rule is broad enough to include adjudicative rules, policy statements, and interpretive rules.

3. Courts require administrative agencies, to the extent possible, to articulate policy by legislative rules using legislative procedures.

4. *Wyman–Gordon* stands for the proposition that the courts will strike down adjudicative rules that are announced prospectively and are not applied in the decisions in which they are announced.

5. Although agencies often try to give adjudicative rules retroactive effect, courts routinely prohibit retroactive application of such rules.

6. Because *Marbury v. Madison* makes it the province of the judiciary to "say what the law is," courts independently determine the meaning of administrative statutes and regulations.

7. *Chevron* deference applies only to administrative interpretations stated in the form of legislative rules.

8. Agencies need to retain the power to articulate policy through the format of adjudicative rules.

9. When an agency articulates policy through informal means (e.g., interpretive statements), and then later reverses course, a court might relieve a regulated entity of the harmful effects (if any) of applying the later interpretation retroactively.

10. Under a long line of precedent, estoppel principles cannot apply against the government.

MULTIPLE CHOICE QUESTIONS

1. In *Chenery II*, the Court suggested which of the following reasons for allowing administrative agencies to articulate policy adjudicatively rather than legislatively:

    A. Problems may arise in a case which the administrative agency could not reasonably foresee, problems which must be solved despite the absence of a relevant general rule.

    B. The agency may not have had sufficient experience with a particular problem to warrant rigidifying its tentative judgment into a hard and fast rule.

    C. The problem may be so specialized and varying in nature as to be impossible of capture within the boundaries of a general rule.

    D. All of the above.

2. Why do some agencies prefer to use adjudicative procedures to articulate policy rather than legislative procedures:

    A. Since adjudicative procedures are not as public, the agency can insulate itself from political pressure.

    B. Congress has expressed a strong preference for adjudicative procedures as a way of making policy.

    C. Courts have urged agencies to use adjudicative procedures because, since those procedures are like procedures used by courts, courts are more comfortable with them.

    D. By creating rules adjudicatively, rather than legislatively, agencies can insulate themselves from judicial review.

3. Which of the following reasons do *not* explain why legislative rulemaking procedures are generally considered preferable to non-legislative procedures for articulating policy:

   A. Since legislative rules generally have prospective effect, whereas adjudicative rules are usually applied retroactively, legislative rules are preferable because they provide regulated entities with notice of regulatory requirements and an opportunity to bring their conduct into compliance.

   B. Since legislative procedures are subject to rulemaking processes (meaning that the agency must announce the proposed rule and give interested parties the opportunity to comment and provide input), they ensure greater public participation and input into the rulemaking process.

   C. Agencies are not the "repositories of all wisdom."

   D. None of the above.

ESSAY QUESTIONS

1. The United States Department of Animal Welfare (DAW) administers the Animal Welfare Act (AWA) which prohibits shippers from transporting animals at "unreasonable" temperatures. A year ago, the DAW issued a press release which stated that it interpreted the term "unreasonable" as including temperatures exceeding 95 degrees. Today, when the temperature is 93 degrees, Ace Animal Shippers (AAS) tries to ship a litter of Golden Retriever puppies through Standiford Field in Louisville, Kentucky. Shortly before the shipment, the DAW made an internal decision to alter its prior interpretation of the AWA. The DAW decided that the term "unreasonable" should be redefined as meaning temperatures exceeding 90 degrees. The DAW notified its inspectors of the new interpretation yesterday, and plans to issue a press release later today. A DAW inspector, noticing that the temperature exceeds 90 degrees, charges the AAS with violating the AWA. Based on the material learned in this chapter, what objections might AAS raise against the citation and what are the chances of success?

2. John Johnson applies for federal crop insurance, and is told that his beet farm is insurable. Johnson duly pays for the insurance for three years. Under the program, Johnson's money is paid into the federal treasury, and payments for

losses come out of the treasury. When Johnson suffers a loss, he files a claim on the federal policy. The federal government denies the claim on the basis that the federal statute that establishes the crop insurance program excludes beet farms. On what basis might you challenge the government's refusal to pay insurance? What are your chances of success?

3. The DAW (referred to in essay #1) decides to promulgate its interpretation—that the term "unreasonable" in the AWA means temperatures exceeding 90 degrees—as a "rule." Would it be preferable for the agency to articulate the new rule using legislative procedures or adjudicative procedures? Why? Explain your reasoning.

ANSWERS TO TRUE–FALSE QUESTIONS

1. False.   Agencies frequently articulate "rules" using notice and comment procedures, but they also do so through non-legislative means, including interpretive rules, policy statements and adjudicative rules.

2. True.   In fact, the definition of a "non-legislative" rule is broad enough to include adjudicative rules, policy statements, and interpretive rules.

3. False.   In decisions like *Chenery II*, the courts have made clear that administrative agencies have discretion about whether to articulate policy legislatively or adjudicatively.

4. False.   Although the *Wyman–Gordon* decision was skeptical regarding the propriety of allowing the NLRB to announce rules for prospective application and not apply them in the cases in which they are announced, the Court ultimately allowed the NLRB to apply the *Excelsior* rule in the *Wyman–Gordon* case.

5. False.   Quite the opposite. Not only do agencies routinely give adjudicative rules retroactive effect, courts often allow them to do so.

6. False.   Although *Marbury v. Madison* gives courts the power to independently determine the meaning of administrative statutes and regulations, courts frequently "defer" to administrative interpretations.

7. False.   In general, the Court has suggested that *Chevron* deference applies only to administrative interpretations stated in the form of legislative rules, but the Court has applied *Chevron* principles to interpretations stated in other formats.

8. True.   In *Chenery II*, the Court made it clear that it would likely be impossible for agencies to articulate all policy through legislative formats, and that agencies must retain the power to articulate policy through the format of adjudicative rules.

9. True.   When an agency articulates policy through informal means (e.g., interpretive statements), and then later reverses course, a court might relieve a regulated entity of the harmful effects (if any) of applying the later interpretation retroactively.

10. False.   While this rule is generally correct, some recent cases have departed from the general rule and allowed the imposition of estoppel principles against the government.

ANSWERS TO MULTIPLE CHOICE QUESTIONS

1. Answer (D), "all of the above," is correct. In *Chenery II*, the Court suggested each of the following reasons for allowing administrative agencies to articulate policy adjudicatively rather than legislatively: Answer (A): "Problems may arise in a case which the administrative agency could not reasonably foresee, problems which must be solved despite the absence of a relevant general rule." Answer (B): "The agency may not have had sufficient experience with a particular problem to warrant rigidifying its tentative judgment into a hard and fast rule." Answer (C) "The problem may be so specialized and varying in nature as to be impossible of capture within the boundaries of a general rule."

2. Answer (A) is correct. Although there are other reasons why agencies prefer to use adjudicative procedures to articulate policy rather than legislative procedures, one reason is Answer (A): "Since adjudicative procedures are not as public, the agency can insulate itself from political pressure." Answer (B) is incorrect because Congress has not expressed a strong preference for adjudicative procedures as a way of making policy. Answer (C) is also incorrect because courts have not urged agencies to use adjudicative procedures on the basis that those procedures are like procedures used by courts and therefore courts are more comfortable with them. Answer (D) is incorrect because, by creating rules adjudicatively, rather than legislatively, agencies cannot insulate themselves from judicial review.

3. Answer (D), "none of the above," is correct because all of the other answers explain why legislative rulemaking procedures are generally considered

preferable to non-legislative procedures for articulating policy, and thus are accurate statements. Thus, Answer (A) is correct: since legislative rules generally have prospective effect, whereas adjudicative rules are usually applied retroactively, legislative rules are preferable because they provide regulated entities with notice of regulatory requirements and an opportunity to bring their conduct into compliance. Answer (B) is also correct: since legislative procedures are subject to rulemaking processes (meaning that the agency must announce the proposed rule and give interested parties the opportunity to comment and provide input), they ensure greater public participation and input into the rulemaking process. Answer (C) is also correct because agencies are not the "repositories of all wisdom."

ANSWERS TO ESSAY QUESTIONS

1. AAS might raise various defenses to the citation. First, it might challenge the agency's interpretation on its face. This challenge is unlikely to succeed because courts are usually deferential to administrative interpretations, and the AWA is clearly ambiguous because it contains the term "unreasonable." Second, AAS might raise a retroactivity challenge against the revised interpretation. The agency's prior interpretation encouraged regulated entities, including AAS, to believe that shipments were permissible at temperatures of 95 degrees or below. When the agency altered its interpretation without giving regulated entities notice, and an opportunity to bring their conduct into compliance, its decision to cite AAS is subject to a retroactivity challenge. AAS is likely to succeed on this challenge. Third, and finally, AAS might challenge the revised interpretation on estoppel grounds. As a general rule, the government cannot be "estopped." However, this case involves an agency that has taken inconsistent positions regarding the meaning of a regulatory provision. In such situations, courts are more likely to "estop" the government although they may not articulate their decision as such.

2. Johnson's chances of success are bleak. The facts of this case are almost identical to those in *Federal Crop Insurance Corp. v. Merrill*. In that case, Merrill argued that, since the Federal Crop Insurance Corp. accepted his premiums and promised to provide him with coverage, it should be estopped from denying that coverage existed. The Court held that the government could not be estopped. The federal statute that authorized the crop insurance program provided the terms under which claims could be paid. Since the money to pay claims would have come from the United States Treasury, the Court held that the Treasury could not be tapped without congressional authorization. Recent decisions have relaxed the notion that the government may not be

estopped, but they continue to apply the rule in cases like this one where money would be spent in contravention of federal authorization.

3.   There is no clear-cut answer to this question. There are strong reasons why agencies should articulate policy legislatively. In general, legislative procedures are considered to be a fairer, and more appropriate, method for making rules for two reasons. First, since legislative rules generally have prospective effect, whereas adjudicative rules are usually applied retroactively, legislative rules provide regulated entities with notice of regulatory requirements and an opportunity to bring their conduct into compliance. Second, since legislative procedures are subject to rulemaking processes (meaning that the agency must announce the proposed rule and give interested parties the opportunity to comment and provide input), they ensure greater public participation and input into the rulemaking process.

At the same time, agencies have reasons for preferring adjudicative procedures for articulating policy. Many administrative agencies prefer to use adjudicative processes to create rules because, since legislative procedures are not as public, the agency can insulate itself from political pressure. When an agency announces a legislative procedure, there is the possibility that various interest groups (e.g., interested national organizations, companies and others) will campaign for or against the rule. By contrast, adjudicative processes are likely to attract less attention. In addition, adjudicative processes are frequently easier and less expensive than national rulemaking proceedings. Finally, adjudicative processes are not subject to many of the procedural requirements applicable to legislative proceedings (e.g., cost-benefit analyses, OMB review, and congressional reviews).

CHAPTER FOUR

The Availability of Judicial Review

A. SEVERAL PREREQUISITES MUST BE MET BEFORE A PARTY CAN OBTAIN JUDICIAL REVIEW

A party seeking judicial review of agency action must satisfy a number of prerequisites before a court can hear its case. This chapter sets forth the most important of these prerequisites.

B. JURISDICTION DOES NOT PRESENT SERIOUS PROBLEMS TODAY

1. Many Organic Statutes Explicitly Confer Jurisdiction

An essential part of obtaining judicial review when a party wishes to challenge a federal agency's action is that the reviewing court have jurisdiction over the case. Article III jurisdiction does not pose a problem, given that challenges to federal agency action arise under federal law. Statutory jurisdiction also does not present a significant problem. Many statutes authorizing administrative action also explicitly confer jurisdiction on a federal court (usually although not always an appellate court) to hear challenges to that action.

2. In the Absence of an Explicit Jurisdictional Grant in the Organic Statute, More Generic Jurisdictional Grants Suffice

When Congress omits such an express jurisdictional grant, more general grants of federal jurisdiction take up the slack. Most helpful is 28 U.S.C.

§ 1331, the general federal question statute, which grants jurisdiction to federal district courts over any case arising under federal law.

3. More General Jurisdictional Grants Give Way to More Specific Ones

However, a general jurisdictional grant may not be used when more specific grants are held to be the exclusive means of obtaining judicial review. For an example, see the Hobbs Act (also known as the Administrative Orders Review Act), 28 U.S.C. § 2342.

4. The APA Does Not Grant Jurisdiction

The APA itself does not grant jurisdiction. Thus, requests for judicial review must rely on either an agency-specific jurisdictional grant or one of the general statutory jurisdictional grants.

C. AGENCY ACTION MUST BE REVIEWABLE BY COURTS

Judicial action must also be reviewable by courts. Courts have interpreted the APA as enacting a broad presumption in favor of judicial review. *See, e.g., Block v. Community Nutrition Institute,* 467 U.S. 340, 104 S.Ct. 2450, 81 L.Ed.2d 270 (1984) (noting this presumption). 5 U.S.C. § 701 provides for judicial review of agency action except "to the extent that (1) statutes preclude judicial review; or (2) agency action is committed to agency discretion by law." These exceptions require separate discussion.

1. Preclusions by Statute Are Normally Construed Narrowly

Except as the Constitution might demand, Congress may make agency actions unreviewable. Courts, however, normally construe such statutory preclusions narrowly, largely to avoid the constitutional issues that might arise were courts completely shut out from being able to review the legality of agency action.

2. Statutory Preclusion Must Be Clear and Convincing

In *Abbott Labs v. Gardner,* 387 U.S. 136, 87 S.Ct. 1507, 18 L.Ed.2d 681 (1967), the Supreme Court stated that the government had to show "clear and convincing evidence" of a congressional intent to preclude review.

3. *Johnson v. Robison* Reflects the "Clear and Convincing" Standard

The Court's insistence on such "clear and convincing" evidence is reflected in *Johnson v. Robison,* 415 U.S. 361, 94 S.Ct. 1160, 39 L.Ed.2d 389 (1974). In *Johnson* the Supreme Court considered a statute that stated "the decisions of the Administrator on any question of law or fact under any law administered by the Veterans' Administration providing benefits for veterans . . . shall be final and conclusive and no . . . court . . . shall have power or jurisdiction to review any such decision." Despite this seemingly clear language, the Court held that Congress did not intend to preclude judicial review of a claim that denial of benefits to a conscientious objector violated his constitutional rights. The Court examined the legislative history of the statute and concluded that it was intended to relieve courts of the duty to review day-to-day benefits decisions made under statutory criteria, and thus also to ensure uniformity of benefits decisions across the nation. According to the Court, however, constitutional claims were different, as they were not within the agency's expertise and were not so numerous as to be burdensome to courts. The Court buttressed its analysis by noting that the statute precluded judicial review of claims *under* any law administered by the agency. These considerations, along with the constitutional questions that would arise should constitutional claims be blocked from judicial review, led the Court to limit the statute's language to precluding review of only such day-to-day claims made pursuant to the statute.

4. Sometimes Statutory Preclusion Is Implicit

Of course, sometimes statutory preclusions of review will prevail. For example, in *Block v. Community Nutrition Institute*, 467 U.S. 340, 104 S.Ct. 2450, 81 L.Ed.2d 270 (1984), the Court found a congressional intent to preclude review of certain agricultural marketing orders at the behest of consumer groups. The Court held that the entire structure of the marketing scheme—in which farmers and wholesalers, but not consumers, were able to participate in the creation of the marketing orders, and in which farmers and wholesalers, but again not consumers, had to go through a detailed administrative dispute resolution process before suing in court—militated against a finding that consumers could sue to challenge those orders.

5. Statutory Preclusion Will Turn on Factors Specific to the Statute

In sum, whether a court will find Congress precluded review of a particular type of agency action will turn on factors particular to the statute, including the nature of the legal claims allegedly precluded, the specificity of the language, and, as in *Block*, the existence of an entire statutory structure that presumes the absence of judicial review of certain claims.

6. The Presumption of Reviewability Remains the Law

While *Block*'s result suggested an erosion of the presumption of reviewability, it explicitly reiterated the existence of that presumption, which should constitute the starting point in any inquiry as to whether Congress has precluded review.

7. "Agency Action Committed to Agency Discretion by Law" Raises Issues

The second exception to reviewability is more opaque than the straightforward (if still difficult) question whether Congress has precluded review by statute. This provision immediately raises two obvious questions: First, what is the difference between preclusion "by law" and preclusion "by statute?" Second, how can agency action be unreviewable because it is "committed to agency discretion" when at the same time courts are empowered under APA § 706 to set aside agency action because it constitutes an abuse of discretion?

8. In *Overton Park*, the Court Described This Exception as Narrow

The modern law of this provision begins with *Citizens to Preserve Overton Park v. Volpe*, 401 U.S. 402, 91 S.Ct. 814, 28 L.Ed.2d 136 (1971). In that case, dealing with a challenge to an agency's decision to route a highway through a city park, the Supreme Court stated that this exception to reviewability was a narrow one, applying only "in those rare instances where statutes are drawn in such broad terms that in a given case there is no law to apply."

9. Agency Decisions Not to Prosecute Are Presumed Unreviewable

The "no law to apply" standard was applied in *Heckler v. Chaney*, 470 U.S. 821, 105 S.Ct. 1649, 84 L.Ed.2d 714 (1985). The Court in that case held that an agency's decision not to prosecute a particular use of a drug as violating federal drug laws, despite a private party's request, was beyond judicial review, as Congress had not prescribed any standards by which the agency was to exercise its prosecutorial discretion.

10. Decisions Not to Prosecute Implicate Judicially Unmanageable Standards

In support of its conclusion, the *Chaney* Court noted the lack of judicially manageable standards for determining the legality of the agency's action, and the resource-allocation issues that go into decisions to prosecute some activities but not others. Those issues, the Court indicated, are best resolved by the agencies themselves, unless Congress prescribes standards that a court can apply.

11. Decisions Not to Institute Rulemakings Are Reviewable

On the other hand, in a widely followed opinion, the D.C. Circuit has held that a court may review an agency's failure to amend a rule in response to a request from an interested party. *American Horse Protection Ass'n v. Lyng*, 812 F.2d 1 (D.C. Cir. 1987).

12. Decisions Not to Institute Rulemakings Implicate Rights Provided in the APA

While decisions to decline to prosecute and to commence a rulemaking may seem similar, they can be distinguished because the APA explicitly authorizes parties to request agencies to initiate a rulemaking process. 5 U.S.C. § 553(e). Because an agency must explain a denial of such a request, the agency decision not to act creates a record that provides a basis for judicial review.

13. Decisions Not to Institute Rulemakings Are Infrequent and Based More Heavily on Legal Considerations

The *American Horse* court also noted that refusals to initiate rulemakings are likely to be relatively infrequent, and to turn more on questions of law, both of which undercut application of *Chaney*'s concerns about standardless judicial intrusion into questions of agency resource allocation.

14. The "No Law to Apply" Standard Has Been Reaffirmed

The Supreme Court, in *Webster v. Doe*, 486 U.S. 592, 108 S.Ct. 2047, 100 L.Ed.2d 632 (1988), reiterated the "no law to apply" rule. In that case the Court refused to hear a claim by a CIA employee that he was fired in contravention of the statute authorizing the Director of the CIA to dismiss employees. Because the statute authorized the Director to dismiss employees *"whenever he shall deem* such termination necessary or advisable in the interests of the United States" (emphasis added), the Court held that the statute provided no judicially cognizable legal standard against which to judge the legality of his action.

15. Constitutional Claims Are Reviewable

However, in *Doe* the Court did hold as reviewable the employee's claim that his dismissal violated his constitutional rights, finding that the Constitution itself provided standards by which to judge the claim.

16. In General, This Exception Remains Narrow

Aside from these relatively unusual cases, however, the rule remains that the "no law to apply" standard is only a narrow exception to the general presumption in favor of judicial review.

D. STANDING REQUIRES A PROPER PLAINTIFF

Standing—the doctrine that examines whether the correct plaintiff is suing—has roots both in Article III of the Constitution's requirement that there be a "case or controversy" and in prudential concerns about the appropriateness of that party as a plaintiff.

1. **Article III Requires Injury, Causation and Redressability**

   Article III of the Constitution limits federal courts' jurisdiction to "cases and controversies." The Supreme Court reads this requirement, in part, as imposing a three part test for standing. In order for a plaintiff to have Article III standing, the plaintiff (1) must be injured, in a way (2) caused by the defendant and (3) redressable by the court.

2. **The Injury Requirement Fulfills the Basic Role of the Courts**

   The Court requires the plaintiff to be injured in order to satisfy the basic idea that the role of Article III courts is to vindicate rights rather than to engage in abstract discussions of law or simply to oversee the workings of the executive branch.

3. **Many Types of Injuries Satisfy the Article III Requirement**

   A broad array of types of injury satisfy this requirement. For example, injury includes not only an impairment of a common-law-protected interest, such as physical integrity, contractual rights, or property, but also impairment of scenic or aesthetic interests.

4. **Congress May Create Rights, the Deprivation of Which Constitutes Article III Injury**

   Moreover, Congress may create rights by statute, the deprivation of which constitutes injury for Article III standing purposes. For example, in the Fair Housing Act of 1968, Congress prohibited the dissemination of false information about the availability of rental housing. When a plaintiff was in fact given such false information and then sued, the Supreme Court, in *Havens Realty v. Coleman*, 455 U.S. 363, 102 S.Ct. 1114, 71 L.Ed.2d 214 (1982), held that the statute had created a right to receive truthful information, which, since it was alleged to have been deprived, supplied the plaintiff with the injury needed for Article III purposes.

5. **The Injury Must Be Imminent or Past**

   However, not all losses satisfy the injury requirement. The Court has required that the injury either have occurred already, or be imminent. For example, in *Lujan v. Defenders of Wildlife*, 504 U.S. 555, 112 S.Ct. 2130, 119 L.Ed.2d 351 (1992), the Court considered a challenge to the government's interpretation of the Endangered Species Act at the behest of professional biologists interested in studying species alleged to be endangered by the government's conduct. The Court rejected the plaintiffs' standing, in part because they had no current plans to travel to the areas where the government's action was alleged to have its extinction-inducing effect. The injury to their professional interests—which the Court stated was the type of harm that would constitute injury—was held to be insufficiently imminent.

6. **Generalized Grievances Do Not Satisfy Article III's Requirements**

   The Court has also insisted that the injury be particularized, rather than a so-called "generalized grievance." Returning to *Defenders*, the plaintiffs also alleged that they were injured because, according to their argument, the statute's grant of a right to sue to "any person" created rights in all persons to have the government act according to law; the deprivation of that right, they claimed, constituted Article III injury. The Court rejected this claim, describing this right as one that inhered in all Americans in equal measure. Thus, the plaintiffs did not suffer some injury particular to them.

7. **Generalized Grievances Are Best Heard by the Political Branches**

   According to the Court, the generalized nature of this grievance rendered their claim more appropriate for consideration by the political branches, rather than by a judiciary whose primary function was to vindicate individual rights.

8. **Ambiguity About the Status of the Generalized Grievance Bar**

   While the *Defenders* Court described the bar on assertion of generalized grievances as based on Article III's constitutional limits, subsequently the Court suggested that the bar was instead merely prudential. *See Federal Election Commission v. Akins*, 524 U.S. 11, 118 S.Ct. 1777, 141 L.Ed.2d 10 (1998).

9. **Mass Tort and Class Action Injuries Are Not Generalized Grievances**

   Note that this analysis does not cast doubt on large, multi-plaintiff litigations such as class actions or mass torts. Those situations are different, because even though many individuals may have suffered an injury, each individual's injury (the impairment of each plaintiff's physical, property, or other interests) was distinct.

10. **Injuries Must Be Caused by the Defendant and Be Redressable by the Court**

    The injury suffered by the plaintiff must also have been caused by the defendant, and must be redressable by the court. Depending on the fact pattern, the causation requirement can constitute a significant hurdle to a plaintiff's standing. Many of the problems revolve around the length of the chain of causation. In many respects, redressability is closely related to causation: if the defendant did not cause the injury, then it is logical to conclude that a court could not redress it.

11. In the 1960's and Early 70's, the Court Entertained More Speculative Causation Links

During the late 1960's and early 1970's the Court was willing to entertain relatively speculative causal links. In the most famous case, *United States v. Students Challenging Regulatory Agency Procedure (SCRAP)*, 412 U.S. 669, 93 S.Ct. 2405, 37 L.Ed.2d 254 (1973), students challenged an Interstate Commerce Commission's rate setting for the hauling of certain types of products that were used in the recycling process. In support of its standing claim, the plaintiffs alleged that they hiked in areas around Washington, D.C., that higher hauling rates for those products would make recycling more expensive and thus less frequent, with the result that more otherwise-recyclable waste would be thrown in the hiking paths, impairing the plaintiffs' recreation. The Court noted the attenuated nature of the causal link, but nevertheless held that the suit could survive a motion to dismiss on the pleadings, and remanded the case to the district court, at which time the plaintiffs would have to produce facts supporting their causation chain. It is doubtful that this case would be decided the same way today.

12. In Later Cases the Court Was Less Willing to Entertain Such Speculative Links

Soon after *SCRAP*, however, the Court began to cut back on its willingness to entertain speculative causation chains. In *Warth v. Seldin*, 422 U.S. 490, 95 S.Ct. 2197, 45 L.Ed.2d 343 (1975), the Court considered a claim that a city's zoning policies unconstitutionally discriminated against the poor, by making it impossible for developers to build low-income housing. The Court held that the plaintiffs failed the causation requirement. It ruled that the plaintiffs could not demonstrate that it was the defendant's zoning policies, rather than the overall economics of the regional housing market, that prevented developers from building low-income housing.

13. Causation and Redressability Play a Special Role in Administrative Law Cases

Causation and redressability have a special role to play in administrative law cases. If the government attempts to accomplish a goal by giving incentives to private parties, then an agency's failure to act according to law might skew those incentives and cause the private party to act in a way harmful to a plaintiff's interests. These kinds of claims, however, raise serious causation and redressability questions.

14. The Court Has Expressed Doubt About Causation in Third Party Cases

For example, in *Simon v. Eastern Kentucky Welfare Rights Org.*, 426 U.S. 26, 96 S.Ct. 1917, 48 L.Ed.2d 450 (1976), the plaintiff alleged that the Internal Revenue Service misread the tax laws by being too lenient in allowing hospitals to retain their charity status while still turning away indigent patients. The plaintiff's injury was that its members were deprived of free medical care that they would otherwise have received from the hospitals. However, the Court held that the plaintiff failed the causation and redressability elements of standing, since the Court could not know whether the regulation caused the plaintiff's injury. The Court reasoned that even in the absence of the (allegedly) overly lenient regulation the hospitals might still consider free care too expensive, and, faced with choosing between providing that care and losing charity status, might opt for the latter. In that case, the regulation would not have caused the injury and, therefore, an injunction against the agency would not redress that injury.

15. Prudential Standing Limits Exist But Can Be Waived

In addition to the Article III requirements discussed above, standing also implicates prudential concerns that inappropriate plaintiffs not bring lawsuits. For example, even when Article III standing requirements are satisfied, a court may still deny standing to a plaintiff when he asserts the legal claim of a third party, on the ground that the right-holder itself is generally the best person to bring the lawsuit. However, because these limitations are not based in the Constitution but rather on prudential concerns, courts and Congress can override them.

16. The APA Sets the Limit for Prudential Standing in Administrative Law Cases

In § 702 of the APA Congress set the prudential standing limit for cases brought under the APA. Section 702 states that a person "suffering legal wrong because of agency action, or adversely affected or aggrieved by agency action within the meaning of a relevant statute" may sue. Because someone whose own legal interests are affected by the action is normally allowed standing anyway, the most important language here is the license to plaintiffs "adversely affected or aggrieved" to sue.

17. The Court Requires Plaintiffs to Be Within the Zone of Interests Protected by the Statute

In *Association of Data Processing Service Organizations v. Camp*, 397 U.S. 150, 90 S.Ct. 827, 25 L.Ed.2d 184 (1970), the Supreme Court interpreted this language as requiring that the plaintiff be "arguably within the zone of interests to be protected by the statute." In *Data Processors,* the plaintiffs alleged that the agency had misread a statute allowing banks to compete with the plaintiffs. The Court held that the plaintiffs were within the zone of interests because the statute was designed in part to limit banks' activities; thus, the Court reasoned that businesses that competed with banks were within the zone.

18. **The Supreme Court Has Held the Zone of Interests Test to Be Not Satisfied in Only One Case**

The only time the Supreme Court has held a plaintiff to fail the zone of interests test was in *Air Courier Conference v. American Postal Workers Union,* 498 U.S. 517, 111 S.Ct. 913, 112 L.Ed.2d 1125 (1991). In that case the postal workers union sued when the agency relaxed its ban on private competition with the postal service. The Court held the union to be outside the zone of interests, because the purpose of Congress in enacting the ban was to protect the postal service's revenues, not postal worker jobs, and because when the relevant statute was enacted in the late 18th century there were no postal workers.

19. **In the *Credit Union* Case, the Court Reiterated the Leniency of the Zone of Interests Test**

In *National Credit Union Admin. v. First National Bank and Trust,* 522 U.S. 479, 118 S.Ct. 927, 140 L.Ed.2d 1 (1998), the Court made clear how lenient the zone of interests test was. In that case the Court considered whether banks were within the zone of interests of a Depression-era statute that limited the scope of individual credit unions. The Court held that the banks were in the zone, reasoning that any statute that limited the competitiveness of credit unions necessarily benefited banks, which competed with them.

20. **The Dissent in *Credit Union* Suggests That the Zone of Interests Test Has Been Eviscerated**

The dissent protested that, when the statute was enacted, banks did not compete for the retail banking market—indeed, that was the very reason Congress enacted legislation allowing credit unions—and thus banks could not have been within the zone.

21. ***Credit Union* Suggests That Competitors Will Always Be Within the Zone of Interests**

The decision in *National Credit Union* strongly suggests that businesses will always be within the zone of interests of a statute that limits their competitors' freedom of action.

22. Only Truly Incidental Beneficiaries Will Fail the Zone of Interests Test

It is difficult to reconcile *Air Courier* and *National Credit Union*. Nevertheless, after *National Credit Union* it seems like the only type of party likely to be held outside of the zone of interest is one who is an utterly incidental beneficiary of a statute. For example, the Court has suggested that a court reporter might have Article III injury if an agency illegally declined to engage in formal, trial-type adjudication, because the agency's action would cause the reporter to lose business. However, the Court suggested that the reporter would be such an obviously incidental beneficiary of the formal hearing requirement that he would be considered outside the zone of interests. *See Lujan v. National Wildlife Federation*, 491 U.S. 871, 883, 110 S.Ct. 3177, 111 L.Ed.2d 695 (1990).

E.   THE LAWSUIT MUST BE PROPERLY TIMED

1.   Courts Try to Avoid Premature Review of Agency Action

Judicial review must be appropriately timed. In general, courts attempt to avoid reviewing agency action before that action is final and before the agency has completed its work.

2.   Avoiding Premature Review Serves Several Functions

This limitation serves several purposes: it allows the agency to apply its full measure of expertise to a problem, ensures the creation of as full a record as possible for judicial review, makes it possible for the agency to correct any mistakes internally, and prevents inappropriate judicial intrusion into an agency's ongoing deliberations. These concerns find expression in three separate, but overlapping doctrines: exhaustion, ripeness, and finality. A final doctrine—primary jurisdiction—also implicates the timing of judicial review.

3.   A Party Must Exhaust Its Administrative Remedies Before Going to Court

The general rule is that private parties must exhaust their administrative remedies before seeking a court's assistance. This rule allows the agency to correct any mistakes it might have made, and promotes respect for agency procedures.

4.   The Exhaustion Requirement Is Highly Discretionary

The exhaustion requirement is highly discretionary, and courts have carved out exceptions to the general exhaustion requirement. Courts have allowed an immediate judicial challenge when it seems clear that an agency has acted beyond its statutory authority. They have also excused a failure to exhaust when the administrative remedy is inadequate. Congress may also influence the exhaustion requirement, for example by doing away with it in certain circumstances.

5. The APA Speaks to Exhaustion

Cases governed by the APA are subject to Section 704's exhaustion requirement. Section 704 provides that a party seeking to appeal an agency decision to a federal court need not first exhaust the agency's internal appeals process unless the agency provides by rule that the appealed decision will be inoperative during the pendency of the internal appeals process. The Supreme Court has held that this provision reflects Congress's decision about exhaustion in cases where that provision applies (*i.e.*, cases governed by the APA); thus, in those cases courts cannot impose additional exhaustion requirements. *Darby v. Cisneros*, 509 U.S. 137, 113 S.Ct. 2539, 125 L.Ed.2d 113 (1993).

6. Agency Action Must Be Ripe

A challenge of an agency action must be ripe for judicial review before a court will hear it. In *Abbott Labs v. Gardner*, 387 U.S. 136, 87 S.Ct. 1507, 18 L.Ed.2d 681 (1967), the Supreme Court held that ripeness requires evaluation of whether (1) the agency action is fit for judicial review at the current time, and (2) the extent to which deferring judicial review would cause significant hardship to the parties.

7. Ripeness as Illustrated in *Abbott Labs*

In *Abbott Labs*, the Court found both of these requirements met, and thus reviewed the legality of an agency's regulation even though it had not yet been enforced against any party. The regulation dealt with labeling requirements for certain health care products, which the private party argued exceeded the agency's statutory authority. The Court held that since the issue was a purely legal one, which further factual development would not illuminate, the action was ripe for judicial review. The Court also noted the hardship to the private party. It had the choice of complying with the regulation and destroying large amounts of existing labels while forgoing any attempt to challenge the regulation, or defying the regulation, in which case it would stand accused of selling adulterated drugs, a charge that might cause it severe harm in the public's mind.

8. Ripeness Is a Function of Both Article III and Prudential Concerns

While the *Abbott Labs* Court was not clear about the genesis of the ripeness requirement, it appears to be a combination of Article III "case or controversy" concerns and prudential concerns. Article III concerns arise when a court is asked to review a decision that is not yet fit for judicial resolution, as it requires a court to engage in abstract speculation that might constitute an advisory opinion. Prudential concerns arise when it's not clear that delaying review would harm anyone.

9. Congress Can Mandate or Prohibit Early Review

Congress can also impact the ripeness inquiry, either by mandating or, conversely, prohibiting judicial review of agency action before any enforcement action is taken against a particular party. For example, in some cases Congress requires that all challenges to an agency regulation be brought within a particular time period after the regulation has been promulgated. Here, though, courts will sometimes make exceptions if after that period has closed the agency enforces the regulation against a party that could not reasonably have foreseen that it could have come within the regulation's ambit. At the other extreme, Congress will sometimes preclude pre-enforcement review of the type allowed in *Abbot Labs*.

10. An Agency Action Must Be Final Before a Court Will Review It

Finally, agency action must be final before it can be challenged in court, unless Congress dispenses with this requirement. Section 704 of the APA provides that "Agency action made reviewable by statute and final agency action for which there is no other adequate remedy in a court are subject to judicial review." The finality requirement serves the purpose of ensuring that the agency has completed its review of the issue and reached an internally authoritative conclusion.

11. Finality Is Determined Based on a Two–Part Test

The Supreme Court has established a two-part test for determining finality. "First, the action must mark the consummation of the agency's decision-making process—it must not be of a merely tentative or interlocutory nature. And second, the action must be one by which rights or obligations have been determined, or from which legal consequences will follow." *Bennett v. Spear*, 520 U.S. 154, 177–178, 117 S.Ct. 1154, 137 L.Ed.2d 281 (1997).

12. The First *Bennett* Prong Illustrated

An earlier appellate court case illustrates the first of these requirements. In *National Automatic Laundry and Cleaning Council v. Shultz*, 443 F.2d 689 (D.C. Cir. 1971), a trade association wrote a letter to an agency, seeking clarification on how it would interpret a particular statute. After receiving the agency's reply, the party sued, claiming that the agency had misread the statute. The court held the suit to be ripe, noting that the letter emanated from a high-level agency official responsible for the administration of the statute, and thus was presumptively the considered opinion of the agency.

13. The Second *Bennett* Prong Illustrated

The second requirement is illustrated by *Bennett* itself. In that case an agency charged with implementing the Endangered Species Act interpreted the statute in a certain way, which authorized a second agency (the "action agency") to take particular actions affecting endangered species. The Court concluded that that interpretation satisfied the second finality element because it altered the legal regime to which the action agency was subject—authorizing the action agency to take certain actions, but only if it complied with the conditions stated in the challenged action.

14. The Doctrine of Primary Jurisdiction Sometimes Delays Judicial Resolution of Suits Between Private Parties

The doctrine of primary jurisdiction arises when two private parties litigate an issue in court that should be passed on first by an administrative agency, in the interest of effective and uniform national regulation. In such a case, the doctrine allows a court to stay its proceedings in order for the relevant agency to examine the facts and make a determination. Of course, after the agency makes that determination, a court is still available to review its correctness within the context of the original private party lawsuit.

15. Primary Jurisdiction Distinguished From Other Timing Limits on Judicial Review

Note that primary jurisdiction is not technically a prerequisite for judicial review of agency action, since it is not one that can be asserted by agencies to avoid judicial review. However, it does affect the ability of a litigant to get judicial review of a claim related to agency action. Moreover, the doctrine's justification—to allow agencies to use their expertise before a court reaches a given issue—reveals its close functional relationship to the timing doctrines discussed above.

16. The Main Candidates for Application of Primary Jurisdiction

Given its justifications, this doctrine is invoked in areas that are heavily regulated in terms of pricing and quality of service, the sort most clearly illustrated by the now-defunct Interstate Commerce Commission's regulation over interstate transportation rates and service. While many such rate regulation schemes have been terminated in the deregulatory movements of the last 30 years, primary jurisdiction remains as a discretionary tool for courts to use in appropriate situations.

TRUE–FALSE QUESTIONS

1. Federal court jurisdiction to review agency actions is provided by the APA.

2. The zone of interests test for standing is a stringent one, which excludes a large number of potential plaintiffs from being able to seek judicial review of agency action.

3. Standing doctrine does not speak to whether the plaintiff's injury can be generalized or whether it has to be particular to her.

4. The APA has been understood to set forth a presumption that agency action is reviewable.

5. The exceptions to the reviewability of agency action have been interpreted to mean more or less the same thing.

6. Agency inaction—whether it be failure to prosecute or failure to initiate a rulemaking—has been held to be unreviewable.

7. The doctrine of primary jurisdiction seeks to ensure that federal courts have the first say at difficult issues of applying regulatory statutes to private party conduct.

8. Ripeness doctrine seeks to determine whether an issue is ripe for judicial resolution at the time of the lawsuit, and whether deferring review would cause a hardship to the parties.

MULTIPLE CHOICE QUESTION

Which of the following statements about standing is true?

A. The zone of interests test seeks to determine whether there is a case or controversy for Article III standing purposes.

B. The Supreme Court has so loosened the requirements for standing that today the doctrine serves more as a pro forma requirement than a real restriction on the availability of judicial review.

C. Standing seeks to ensure that the agency have the initial opportunity to decide an issue before a court does.

D. The zone of interests test restricts very few types of injured plaintiffs from being able to sue.

ESSAY QUESTION

The government plans to build an oil pipeline through a wildlife area serving as the last remaining habitat of an endangered species. The following people wish to sue, alleging a violation of the Endangered Species Act: (1) A biologist who generally studies the species but who does not currently have a research plan or current plans to see the species in the wild; (2) A tourist who has booked a safari where he hopes to see the species in the wild; and (3) A member of the public who is offended at the thought that the government might be violating the Endangered Species Act? Which of these plaintiffs might be held to have standing?

ANSWERS TO TRUE–FALSE QUESTIONS

1. False.   The APA does not provide jurisdiction. Jurisdiction can be found either in the agency's authorizing statute, or, if not provided there, in more general jurisdictional grants, most notably the general federal question jurisdiction grant of 28 U.S.C. § 1331.

2. False.   The zone of interests test, as interpreted in *National Credit Union*, is extremely broad, excluding at most only those plaintiffs who are utterly incidental beneficiaries under a statute.

3. False.   While it is not completely clear whether the bar on assertion of generalized grievances rests on Article III or simply constitutes a prudential limitation, there are limits on the ability of a party to assert a generalized grievance.

4. True.   Section 701 of the APA has been interpreted to set forth a presumption of reviewability.

5. False.   The exception for statutory preclusion looks primarily at congressional intent, while the exception for "agency action committed to agency discretion by law" has been understood to refer to situations where the statute is written so broadly that there is no law to apply.

6. False.   While in *Heckler v. Chaney* the Court held that agency failures to prosecute are presumptively unreviewable, lower courts have held that agency failures to initiate a rulemaking are subject to judicial review.

7. False.   Primary jurisdiction has as its purpose ensuring that agencies are able to bring their expertise to bear on complex regulatory issues *before* a court faces them.

8. True.   In *Abbott Labs v. Gardner* the Court enunciated that test for ripeness.

ANSWER TO MULTIPLE CHOICE QUESTION

The correct answer is (D). After *National Credit Union*, almost anyone who satisfies the Article III standing test would satisfy the zone of interests requirement. (A) is incorrect: the zone of interests test is a prudential limit on standing, rather than one based in Article III's case or controversy requirement. (B) is incorrect because, while the zone of interests test has become significantly loosened in recent years, the Court's Article III standing requirements have, if anything, been tightened. (C) is incorrect; standing does not deal with the timing of judicial review, but instead deals with the question of which parties can trigger judicial review.

ANSWER TO ESSAY QUESTION

Only the tourist would have standing. The tourist's recreational interests are of the type that the Court has recognized as cognizable for Article III injury purposes. Moreover, his injury can be thought of as imminent, since he has concrete plans to visit an area where the species lives. By contrast, the biologist does not have such concrete plans; in *Defenders of Wildlife* the Court denied standing to a party like this because her injury was not sufficiently imminent and concrete. The member of the public suffers a generalized grievance; such a standing theory was also rejected in *Defenders of Wildlife*.

CHAPTER FIVE

Inspections, Reports & Subpoenas

A. INTRODUCTION

Administrative agencies thrive on information. They use information to set policy through the promulgation of rules and regulations, to keep Congress advised regarding various matters, and to enforce regulatory requirements and prosecute companies for civil and criminal violations. Agencies obtain this information in different ways: they conduct inspections and searches; they require persons to submit information or produce documents to the agency; and they require persons to keep records which the government is allowed to inspect. This chapter considers the legal and constitutional authority of agencies to acquire information, the role of agency lawyers in authorizing such action, and what steps lawyers who represent individuals or companies can take to limit such efforts.

B. INSPECTIONS

A number of agencies regularly inspect buildings and work sites. Health inspectors enter restaurants to determine whether food preparation and service areas are clean, as well as to see whether food is being kept under healthy conditions. Inspectors from the Occupational Safety and Health Administration (OSHA) examine construction and factory sites to make sure that workers are employed in safe and healthy conditions. In some instances, administrative officials even seek to enter people's homes or yards. Child welfare officials, for example, enter homes looking for abused or neglected children.

1. Legal Authority to Inspect

An agency's authority to inspect is defined by its enabling act. If Congress (or a state legislature) has not authorized an agency to conduct administrative inspections, it has no legal authority to do so. Moreover, an agency's authority to inspect is co-extensive with its statutory authorization.

2. Fourth Amendment Limitations

As we shall see, agency authority to inspect is also limited by the Fourth Amendment which provides that: "The right of the people to be secure in their persons, houses, papers, and effects, against unreasonable searches and seizures, shall not be violated, and no Warrants shall issue, but upon probable cause, supported by Oath or affirmation, and particularly describing the place to be searched, and the persons or things to be seized." U.S. Const. Amend IV. Through the Fourteenth Amendment, state agencies are also subject to the Fourth Amendment.

a. Prior Precedent Regarding the Fourth Amendment

Until the 1960s, there was doubt about whether the Fourth Amendment required a warrant for administrative inspections. For example, in *Frank v. Maryland*, 359 U.S. 360, 79 S.Ct. 804, 3 L.Ed.2d 877 (1959), the Supreme Court held that the warrant requirement did not apply to administrative inspections because they "touch at most upon the periphery of the important interests safeguarded by the Fourteenth Amendment's protection against official intrusion."

b. Camara v. Municipal Court

However, in *Camara v. Municipal Court*, 387 U.S. 523, 87 S.Ct. 1727, 18 L.Ed.2d 930 (1967), the Court overruled *Frank* and held that the Fourth Amendment applies to administrative inspections. *Camara* involved a San Francisco ordinance that made it illegal to refuse to permit an inspection under the municipal code. When a homeowner refused to permit an inspector to enter his residence, he was charged with violating the ordinance. The Court held that the homeowner was protected under the Fourth Amendment: "[The Fourth Amendment was designed] to safeguard the privacy and security of individuals against arbitrary invasions by governmental officials. [E]xcept in certain carefully defined classes of cases, a search of private property without proper consent is "unreasonable" unless it has been authorized by a valid search warrant. [W]e hold that administrative searches of the kind at issue here are significant intrusions upon the interests protected by the Fourth Amendment, that such searches when authorized and conducted without a warrant procedure lack the traditional safeguards which the Fourth Amendment guarantees to the individual. [Because] of the nature of the municipal programs under consideration, however, these conclusions must be the beginning, not the end, of our inquiry."

c.   Warrant Requirement

Camara also made clear that, in the administrative context, the Fourth Amendment requires the government to obtain a warrant based on "probable cause." Absent a warrant, or the consent of the property owner (or some other exception to the warrant requirement), a search is deemed to be "unreasonable" and therefore invalid under the Fourth Amendment.

d.   The Requirement of Probable Cause

Although *Camara* held that a warrant must be based on "probable cause," the court redefined the concept. Traditionally, the probable cause requirement requires particularized proof focusing on the individual or place to be search. The Court recognized that this standard does not work well in the administrative context because the "only effective way to seek universal compliance with the minimum standards required by municipal codes is through routine periodic inspections of all struc- tures." As a result, the Court held that the warrant requirement would not be specifically applied in the administrative context and might be satisfied by so-called "area inspections" even though "such inspections are 'unavoidably based on its [the agency's] appraisal of conditions in the area as a whole, not on its knowledge of conditions in each particular building.' "

e.   Support for Area Inspections

Camara further justified "area inspections" on the following grounds: "[W]e think that a number of persuasive factors combine to support the reasonableness of area code-enforcement inspections. First, such pro- grams have a long history of judicial and public acceptance. Second, the public interest demands that all dangerous conditions be prevented or abated, yet it is doubtful that any other canvassing technique would achieve acceptable results. Many such conditions—faulty wiring is an obvious example—are not observable from outside the building and indeed may not be apparent to the inexpert occupant himself. Finally, because the inspections are neither personal in nature nor aimed at the discovery of evidence of crime, they involve a relatively limited invasion of the urban citizen's privacy."

f.   "Reasonable" Legislative or Administrative Standards

In general, the Court has focused on whether the agency has established "reasonable legislative or administrative standards" for conducting inspections under the regulatory scheme. For building inspections, the Court concluded that "[s]uch standards, which will vary with the municipal program being enforced, may be based upon the passage of time, the nature of the building (*e.g.*, a multifamily apartment house), or the condition of the entire area, but they will not necessarily depend upon specific knowledge of the condition of the particular dwelling."

g.   Permissible Grounds for Warrantless Inspections

Despite the Court's preference for a warrant, the Court recognized that warrantless inspections have traditionally been upheld in a variety of contexts including "emergency situations. *See North American Cold Storage Co. v. City of Chicago*, 211 U.S. 306, 29 S.Ct. 101, 53 L.Ed. 195 (1908) (seizure of unwholesome food); *Jacobson v. Commonwealth of Massachusetts*, 197 U.S. 11, 25 S.Ct. 358, 49 L.Ed. 643 (1905) (compulsory smallpox vaccination); *Compagnie Francaise de Navigation a Vapeur v. Louisiana State Board of Health*, 186 U.S. 380, 22 S.Ct. 811, 46 L.Ed. 1209 (1902) (health quarantine); *Kroplin v. Truax*, 119 Ohio St. 610, 165 N.E. 498 (1929) (summary destruction of tubercular cattle)." However, the Court noted that routine area inspections do not present emergency or exigent circumstances.

h.   *Camara's* Extension to Businesses

In *See v. City of Seattle*, 387 U.S. 541, 87 S.Ct. 1737, 18 L.Ed.2d 943 (1967), *Camara's* holding was extended to inspections of commercial properties. The Court held that a "businessman, like the occupant of a residence, has a constitutional right to go about his business free from unreasonable official entries upon his private property." In later cases, the warrant requirement has been extended to a variety of other administrative inspections.

i.   Closely Regulated Businesses

Following *Camara*, the Court recognized an exception from the warrant requirement for businesses and industries that had long been subject to close government regulation. The theory was that a person entering such a business had a reduced expectation of privacy. *See Colonnade Catering Corp. v. United States*, 397 U.S. 72, 90 S.Ct. 774, 25 L.Ed.2d 60 (1970) (liquor dealers); *United States v. Biswell*, 406 U.S. 311, 92 S.Ct. 1593, 32 L.Ed.2d 87 (1972) (firearms dealers); *Donovan v. Dewey*, 452 U.S. 594, 101

S.Ct. 2534, 69 L.Ed.2d 262 (1981) (underground mines); *New York v. Burger*, 482 U.S. 691, 107 S.Ct. 2636, 96 L.Ed.2d 601 (1987) (auto junkyard). In regard to such businesses, the Court asked first whether the searches serve an important government purpose and are necessary to achieve that purpose. The Court also inquired whether the statute authorizing the searches provides protections substituting for a warrant—providing notice of searches to the owner, limiting the scope of the search, and limiting the discretion of the inspecting officer.

j. OSHA Inspections

In *Marshall v. Barlow's, Inc.*, 436 U.S. 307, 98 S.Ct. 1816, 56 L.Ed.2d 305 (1978), the Court refused to extend the "closely regulated business" exception to businesses subject to the Occupational Safety and Health Act. The Court concluded that application of the exception to OSHA inspections would create a gaping hole in Fourth Amendment protections since virtually every industry in the United States is subject to OSHA. In addition, the Court doubted that the warrant requirement would "impose serious burdens on the inspection system or the courts, [would] prevent inspections necessary to enforce the statute, or [would] make them less effective. In the first place, the great majority of businessmen can be expected in the normal course to consent to inspection without warrant."

k. Administrative Inspections and Consent

Even though *Camara* imposes a warrant requirement, the reality is that most administrative inspections are conducted without a warrant by the consent of the parties. Most businesses recognize that there is little to be gained by refusing consent in the ordinary situation. If consent is refused, the inspector will most likely return with a warrant, but may not be in the best of humor and may be more likely to find violations. For these reasons, many industry groups advise their members to willingly consent to administrative inspections.

l. The *Burger* Exception

In *New York v. Burger*, 482 U.S. 691, 107 S.Ct. 2636, 96 L.Ed.2d 601 (1987), the Court extended the "closely regulated industry" exception to what seemed like traditional criminal conduct. That case involved the New York Vehicle and Traffic Law which provided that persons engaged in the business of vehicle dismantling were required to have a license and to keep records of the vehicles coming into their possession. The law further provided that "[u]pon request of an agent of the commissioner or of any police officer and during his regular and usual business hours, a vehicle dismantler shall produce such records and permit said agent or police officer to examine them and any vehicles or parts of vehicles which are subject to the record keeping requirements." The statute did not require a warrant. The law was applied to Burger who ran an automobile junkyard and who was raided by New York police who suspected him of running a "chop shop," a place where stolen cars are dismantled for parts. The police found stolen cars on the premises and Burger was convicted of possession of stolen property. The Court rejected Burger's claim that the search was unconstitutional, concluding that there was no constitutional significance to the fact that police undertook the inspections or that they might find evidence of crime in addition to evidence of regulatory violations (such as a failure to have a license or keep appropriate records). "So long as a regulatory scheme is properly administrative, it is not rendered illegal by the fact that the inspecting officer has the power to arrest individuals for violations other than those created by the scheme itself."

3. Remedies for Illegal Inspections

Even though *Camara* loosened the probable cause requirements for administrative searches, illegal inspections do occur. Sometimes, an agency obtains a warrant but the warrant is invalidly issued. In other cases, as in *Barlow's*, the agency searches without a warrant when one is required. In addition, the police may conduct an illegal search and give the results to administrative officials. In these contexts, remedial questions arise.

a. Monetary Remedies

When governmental officials illegally enter a home or business, they may be subjected to various remedies. For example, they be liable in tort under state law (e.g., trespass) or held liable under federal law. When federal, state, or local officials violate a citizen's Fourth Amendment right to be free from unreasonable searches and seizures, they can also be sued under the Constitution itself, *Bivens v. Six Unknown Named Agents of the Federal Bureau of Narcotics*, 403 U.S. 388, 91 S.Ct. 1999, 29 L.Ed.2d 619 (1971) (petitioner entitled to sue federal officials for violating his Fourth Amendment rights), or under 42 U.S.C.A. § 1983 (authorizing suits against state officials who infringe citizens' "rights, privileges, or immunities secured by the Constitution and laws" of the United States).

b. The Exclusionary Evidence Rule

Another potential remedy is the exclusionary evidence rule. The federal courts have long prohibited federal prosecutors from using evidence seized in violation of a defendant's constitutional rights in criminal cases. *Weeks v. United States*, 232 U.S. 383, 34 S.Ct. 341, 58 L.Ed. 652 (1914). In *Mapp v. Ohio*, 367 U.S. 643, 81 S.Ct. 1684, 6 L.Ed.2d 1081 (1961), the Court extended this rule to state prosecutions. However, neither decision applied the exclusionary rule to deny administrative agencies the use of information in administrative cases.

4. United States v. Janis

In *United States v. Janis*, 428 U.S. 433, 96 S.Ct. 3021, 49 L.Ed.2d 1046 (1976), the Court refused to apply the exclusionary rule in a civil proceeding when evidence was seized in good faith by criminal law enforcement officials who were found to have acted unconstitutionally. In concluding that the evidence was admissible the Court balanced the "benefit" of exclusion (which it defined as the hope that exclusion will deter the police from future misconduct), against the "costs" (which it defined as the loss of evidence), and concluded that the evidence should be admitted. The Court concluded that the police were already deterred by their inability to use the seized evidence in a criminal prosecution, and it doubted that the deterrent effect was enhanced by exclusion of the evidence from civil proceedings.

5. Intra–Agency Exclusion and Deterrence

Although *Janis* refused to apply the exclusionary rule in a civil context, the decision did not rule out the possibility that the rule might be applied in civil proceedings when the deterrent effect of exclusion might be served. One of the motivating factors behind the *Janis* decision was the idea that the evidence had been seized by the police for use in criminal proceedings. The Court concluded that the police are motivated to obtain illegal evidence for use in criminal proceedings, but are not motivated by the possibility of using the evidence in civil proceedings. As a result, *Janis* left open the possibility that the exclusionary rule might be applied when administrative officials seized evidence for use in civil proceedings. In that intra-agency use of illegal evidence, application of the exclusionary rule might deter future governmental misconduct.

6. INS v. Lopez–Mendoza

However, in *INS v. Lopez–Mendoza*, 468 U.S. 1032, 104 S.Ct. 3479, 82 L.Ed.2d 778 (1984), the Court refused to apply the exclusionary evidence rule in an intra-agency context. That case involved unique facts and probably does not doom all future intra-agency applications of the rule. In *Lopez–Mendoza*, a suspect admitted that he was an illegal alien during an illegal arrest. When the Immigration and Naturalization Service (INS) sought to use the admission in a deportation proceeding, the suspect moved to exclude the evidence. Nevertheless, the Court concluded that the "likely deterrent value of the exclusionary rule in a civil deportation proceeding" was limited. The Court noted that, "regardless of how the arrest is effected, deportation will still be possible when evidence not derived directly from the arrest is sufficient to support deportation." The Court noted that the suspect's person and identity are not suppressible, and the INS need only prove alienage, something that it can do using other evidence. The Court also expressed other concern about whether exclusion would deter INS agents in this unique context.

C. "SPECIAL NEEDS" SEARCHES

Many administrative agencies also conduct so-called "special needs" searches and the Court has dispensed with both the warrant requirement and the probable cause requirement. Illustrative are the imposition of mandatory drug tests for employees and students. As is the case with inspections, the question arises whether drug tests can be required absent a particularized showing of probable cause that would justify a warrant. Many of these searches have been upheld.

1. "Need" Versus "Intrusion" Test

The Fourth Amendment prohibits "unreasonable" searches and seizures. In *Camara v. Municipal Court*, as we saw, the Court held that warrantless administrative inspections are "unreasonable" and therefore unconstitutional. In the special needs context, the Court has continued to focus on the Fourth Amendment requirement of reasonableness. However, in deciding whether it is "reasonable" for an agency to proceed without a warrant and whether it can also dispense with the requirement of probable cause, the Court balances the "need" for the search against the level of "intrusion" caused thereby.

2. The *Skinner* Decision

In *Skinner v. Railway Labor Executives' Association*, 489 U.S. 602, 109 S.Ct. 1402, 103 L.Ed.2d 639 (1989), the Court upheld Federal Railroad Administration (FRA) regulations mandating blood and urine testing of railroad employees involved in "major" train accidents, and authorizing railroads to administer breath and urine tests to employees who violate certain safety rules. The Court upheld the regulations noting that the "governmental interest in ensuring the safety of the traveling public and of the employees themselves plainly justifies prohibiting covered employees from using alcohol or drugs on duty, or while subject to being called for duty." The Court emphasized that "[A]lcohol and other drugs are eliminated from the bloodstream at a constant rate, and blood and breath samples taken to measure whether these substances were in the bloodstream when a triggering event occurred must be obtained as soon as possible. [T]he delay necessary to procure a warrant nevertheless may result in the destruction of valuable evidence." As a result, the Court concluded that the "Government interest in testing without a showing of individualized suspicion is compelling." Finally, the Court held that covered employees had a diminished expectation of privacy due to the nature of their jobs, and that the "the privacy interests implicated by the search were minimal" because of the manner in which the tests were performed.

3. *Earls* and Drug Testing of Students

In *Board of Education of Independent School District No. 92 of Pottawatomie County v. Earls*, 536 U.S. 822, 122 S.Ct. 2559, 153 L.Ed.2d 735 (2002), the Court extended the special needs exception to a high school program involving suspicionless, warrantless, drug testing of students involved in extra-curricular activities. The Court concluded that the need for such searches was great given the drug epidemic in the United States. In addition, the court found that the intrusion was not severe given the way the urine samples were collected (a student was allowed to go into a private booth and the teacher waited outside listening for sounds of urination), and the general confidentiality with which they were kept. In addition, test results were not revealed to law enforcement authorities, but were only used to determine whether students could participate in extra-curricular activities. The Court upheld the program: "Given the minimally intrusive nature of the sample collection and the limited uses to which the test results are put, we conclude that the invasion of students' privacy is not significant. . . . Given the nationwide epidemic of drug use, and the evidence of increased drug use in Tecumseh schools, it was entirely reasonable for the School District to enact this particular drug testing policy."

4. *Ferguson* & Drug Testing for Pregnant Women

In *Ferguson v. City of Charleston*, 532 U.S. 67, 121 S.Ct. 1281, 149 L.Ed.2d 205 (2001), a city instituted a program whereby the local hospital, without the knowledge or consent of the patients, would perform drug screens on the urine samples provided by pregnant patients and, if the drug test was positive, the hospital would provide the results to local law enforcement. Then, depending upon the stage of their pregnancy, the patients were either arrested for child abuse or given the opportunity to avoid criminal prosecution by successfully completing a drug counseling program. The Court by a 6–3 margin found that the program violated the Fourth Amendment. Comparing the program to other urine testing cases, the Court stressed that in all the other cases the subjects were aware of the drug testing of their urine, and in a sense their submission to the testing was voluntary, because they could avoid it by avoiding the triggering activity. In addition, the Court emphasized that none of the other cases involved use of the results for law enforcement purposes.

D. RECORDKEEPING AND REPORTING REQUIREMENTS

Agencies also require individuals and corporations to keep and report information for a variety of purposes and in a variety of manners.

1. Collection of Statistical Data

Some agencies gather statistics. For example, the United States Department of Commerce's Bureau of the Census conducts a decennial census mandated by the Constitution, and also conducts more targeted data collections as required by Congress (e.g., to monitor the economy). The United States Department of Engery's Energy Information Administration collects data regarding oil imports into the United States.

2. Regulatory Monitoring

Agencies also gather information to monitor compliance with their regulatory programs. For instance, under the Clean Water Act, those who hold permits to discharge pollutants must submit monitoring reports. Agencies also gather information to help them determine whether statutes or regulations have been violated, or to gather evidence to proceed against violators. For example, taxpayers are required to report their annual income on their tax returns.

3. Imposition by Regulation

Recordkeeping and reporting requirements are usually imposed by regulation, but some reporting requirements are informally imposed by agencies (e.g., by letter). Usually, in order to impose a recordkeeping or reporting requirement, the agency must find statutory authority, implicit or explicit. If an agency decides to impose a reporting or recordkeeping requirement by regulation, it must comply with the APA's rulemaking processes.

4. Imposition by Other Means

In *In re FTC Line of Business Report Litigation*, 595 F.2d 685 (D.C.Cir.1978), the court held that not all recordkeeping and reporting requirements must be imposed by regulation. That case involved the FTC's attempt to impose a "Line of Business" (LB) survey on large domestic manufacturing concerns, and its Corporate Patterns Report (CPR) on 1100 large corporations, in an attempt to develop data on market structures that could be used for various purposes (e.g., antitrust enforcement, economic analysis, and policy planning). The Court upheld the survey requirements: "[T]he Administrative Procedure Act does not independently require rulemaking prior to the issuance of FTC informational report orders. The language and legislative history of the APA suggest a classification of agency activity into three basic categories: rulemaking, adjudication and investigation. The issuance of agency orders to compel the filing of informational reports was plainly regarded an investigative act by the drafters of the APA, not a rule or adjudication. . . . In this case, the enabling statutory provision is Section 6(b) of the FTC Act, which [does] not impose rulemaking upon the FTC. Accordingly, the Commission is not obligated under the Administrative Procedure Act to pursue rulemaking proceedings prior to implementation of the LB and CPR programs. . . . The Federal Trade Commission Act (FTC Act) provides a clear basis of authority for the Commission to issue orders requiring corporations to submit informational reports to the FTC."

5. The Paperwork Reduction Act

The Paperwork Reduction Act. 44 U.S.C.A. §§ 3501 *et seq.*, imposes limitations on agencies that seek to impose reporting or recordkeeping requirements on 10 or more persons. However, the Act is subject to various exemptions. 44 U.S.C.A. § 3502(3).

a. Oversight Office

The Act requires agencies to establish offices to oversee information collection. 44 U.S.C.A. § 3506(a)(2). When an agency proposes to collect information, the oversight office must review the request and evaluate the agency's asserted need as well as the plan details. 44 U.S.C.A. § 3506(c)(1). In addition the office must estimate the amount of burden imposed by the collection requirement. Id. If the agency does not proceed by rulemaking, the office must publish the collection requirement in the *Federal Register* and accept comments. Once the comments are received, the office must certify that the information collection is necessary, is not duplicative of other information available to the agency, reduces the burden on small entities, is written understandably, is implemented consistently with existing reporting and recordkeeping practices, indicates the amount of time required to comply, and has been developed in a way designed to produce efficient and effective management and use of the information collected, uses effective and efficient statistical survey methodology, and uses information technology to reduce the burden and improve data quality, agency efficiency and responsiveness to the public. 44 U.S.C.A. § 3506(3).

b.   OIRA Review

After the internal agency office conducts its review, the agency must submit its proposed collection requirement to the Office of Management and Budget's (OMB) Office of Information and Regulatory Affairs (OIRA). 44 U.S.C.A. § 3507(a)(1)(C). The proposal must then be published in the *Federal Register*, and OIRA must wait at least thirty days before approving the request, and must approve or disapprove the request within 60 days based on whether "the collection of information by the agency is necessary for the proper performance of the functions of the agency." 44 U.S.C.A. § 3508.

c.   OIRA and Agency Rulemakings

If the agency opts to impose an information collection requirement by rule, OIRA participates in the rulemaking process by submitting comments. 44 U.S.C.A. § 3507(d). If OIRA finds that the agency's response to its comments are "unreasonable," OIRA has 60 days to disapprove the rule. However, when OIRA disapproves a request from an independent regulatory agency, the members can override the OIRA decision by majority vote. 44 U.S.C.A. § 3507(f). The agency head can circumvent these processes, and seek immediate approval, if he/she determines that there is an "emergency." 44 U.S.C.A. § 3507(j).

d.   Control Numbers

If OIRA approves an information collection request, OIRA provides a mandatory "control number" for the request. 44 U.S.C.A. § 3507(a)(3). If an information collection document does not contain a control number, or a required notice regarding the obligation to complete, those who refuse to comply cannot be penalized for failure to provide the requested information. 44 U.S.C.A. § 3512.

e.   Paperwork Reduction Act Exemptions

The Paperwork Reduction Act does not apply to federal criminal investigations, to judicial actions to which the United States or an agency is a party, during an administrative action or investigation directed against specific persons, to functions performed by intelligence agencies, or by compulsory process under the Antitrust Civil Process Act or Section 13 of the Federal Trade Commission Improvements Act.

f. Judicial Review

An OIRA decision to approve an information collection is exempt from judicial review. 44 U.S.C.A. § 3507(d)(6).

E. SUBPOENAS AND THE FOURTH AMENDMENT

Early court decisions limited the power of administrative agencies to obtain information by subpoena. *See Federal Trade Commission v. American Tobacco Co.*, 264 U.S. 298, 44 S.Ct. 336, 68 L.Ed. 696 (1924). However, in *Oklahoma Press Publishing Co. v. Walling*, 327 U.S. 186, 66 S.Ct. 494, 90 L.Ed. 614 (1946), the Court held that an agency may subpoena information even if it lacks "probable cause." The Court found that a probable cause requirement "would stop much if not all of the investigation in the public interest at the threshold of the inquiry."

1. Requirement to "Particularly Describe"

In *Oklahoma Press*, instead of probable cause, the Court held that "[T]he Fourth [Amendment] at most guards against abuse only by way of too much indefiniteness or breadth in the things required to be 'particularly described,' if also the inquiry is one the demanding agency is authorized by law to make and the materials specified are relevant. The gist of the protection is in the requirement, expressed in terms, that the disclosure shall not be unreasonable."

2. "Fishing Expeditions?"

United States v. Morton Salt Co., 338 U.S. 632, 70 S.Ct. 357, 94 L.Ed. 401 (1950), involved an agency's attempt to impose a reporting requirement on regulated entities. The Court rejected the company's assertion that the reporting requirement involved nothing more than a "fishing expedition" and therefore that production should not be required: "[Because] judicial power is reluctant if not unable to summon evidence until it is shown to be relevant to issues in litigation, it does not follow that an administrative agency charged with seeing that the laws are enforced may not have and exercise powers of original inquiry. It has a power of inquisition, if one chooses to call it that, which is not derived from the judicial function. It is more analogous to the Grand Jury, which does not depend on a case or controversy for power to get evidence but can investigate merely on suspicion that the law is being violated, or even just because it wants assurance that it is not. . . . Of course a government investigation into corporate matters may be of such a sweeping nature and so unrelated to the matter under inquiry as to exceed the investigatory power. But it is sufficient if the inquiry is within the authority of the agency, the demand is not too indefinite and the information sought is reasonably relevant."

3. *Whalen* and Privacy Issues

In *Whalen v. Roe*, 429 U.S. 589, 97 S.Ct. 869, 51 L.Ed.2d 64 (1977), plaintiffs objected on privacy grounds to a New York statute that required physicians to submit drug prescription information to the state. Although the Court rejected plaintiffs' privacy claim, on the basis that only a few governmental officials had access to the information, the Court suggested that a privacy claim might limit reporting requirements in appropriate cases: "[We] are not unaware of the threat to privacy implicit in the accumulation of vast amounts of personal information in computerized data banks or other massive government files. . . . The right to collect and use such data for public purposes is typically accompanied by a concomitant statutory or regulatory duty to avoid unwarranted disclosures."

F. THE FIFTH AMENDMENT AND COMPELLED DISCLOSURES

In addition to Fourth Amendment constraints on governmental information collections, litigants sometimes challenge collections under the Fifth Amendment privilege against self-incrimination, which provides that no person "shall be compelled in any criminal case to be a witness against himself. . . . " U.S. Const. Amend V.

1. Application to Administrative Proceedings

Although the privilege against self-incrimination precludes incrimination in a criminal proceeding, testimony at civil or administrative proceedings can be criminally incriminating. In other words, statements made in administrative proceedings might be used to prosecute individuals in later criminal proceedings. As a result, the privilege applies to statements made in administrative proceedings which might be used against witnesses in subsequent or parallel criminal proceedings.

2. Prohibition Against "Testimonial" Self–Incrimination

In general, the privilege against self-incrimination protects witnesses only against compelled testimonial self-incrimination. In other words, witnesses can be protected against being forced to testify against themselves. The privilege generally does not protect witnesses against a requirement to produce documents.

3. Inapplicability to Corporations

In addition, the privilege only protects natural persons, and does not protect corporations or unincorporated associations. *See United States v. White*, 322 U.S. 694, 64 S.Ct. 1248, 88 L.Ed. 1542 (1944) (labor union denied privilege against self-incrimination); *Hale v. Henkel*, 201 U.S. 43, 26 S.Ct. 370, 50 L.Ed.

652 (1906) (a "corporation is a creature of the state. . . . " and "[i]t would be a strange anomaly to hold that a state, having chartered a corporation to make use of certain franchises, could not, in the exercise of its sovereignty, inquire how these franchises had been employed, and whether they had been abused, and demand the production of the corporate books and papers for that purpose. . . . ").

4. Inapplicability to Corporate and Associational Documents

Given that the privilege against self-incrimination does not protect corporations, and applies only to testimony and not to documents, the privilege does not protect corporate books and records. As a result, even if a natural person is heavily involved with the production of those documents, and therefore might be incriminated by production, corporate documents must still be produced. Of course, if the corporate custodian cannot produce the documents without incriminating him/herself, he/she is entitled to assert the privilege on behalf of him/herself. Nevertheless, the corporation must still produce the documents, and must appoint another corporate agent (presumably, one who will not incriminate him/herself in producing them) to make the production. *See Wilson v. United States*, 221 U.S. 361, 31 S.Ct. 538, 55 L.Ed. 771 (1911).

5. Inapplicability to "Required Records"

In *Shapiro v. United States*, 335 U.S. 1, 68 S.Ct. 1375, 92 L.Ed. 1787 (1948), the Court refused to apply the privilege to "required records" which the government requires an individual to keep "in order that there may be suitable information of transactions which are the appropriate subjects of government regulation and the enforcement of restrictions validly established."

6. Inapplicability to Other Documents

Because the privilege against self-incrimination protects only "testimony" and not documents, it does not protect incriminating documents held by an individual. *See United States v. Doe*, 465 U.S. 605, 104 S.Ct. 1237, 79 L.Ed.2d 552 (1984). This is true even for highly personal documents (e.g., a personal diary).

7. Registration Requirements

The privilege also applies when the government or an agency of government requires an individual to register under circumstances which might be incriminating. *See Marchetti v. United States*, 390 U.S. 39, 88 S.Ct. 697, 19 L.Ed.2d 889 (1968) (requirement that anyone involved in the business of accepting bets must register as an illegal bookie is unconstitutional where the act of registering essentially admits an illegal act).

8.   Incriminating Acts of Production

The privilege might also apply to the production of documents when the "act" of production would, itself, be incriminating. Suppose, for example, that the government demands production of "incriminating documents indicating that defendant engaged in tax fraud," as opposed to demanding production "of all tax documents in defendant's possession." In the former situation, if the defendant produces the documents, he/she essentially admits that the produced documents are incriminating. In such situations, the defendant can simply assert the privilege against self-incrimination as a bar to production or reporting. *See United States v. Doe*, 465 U.S. 605, 104 S.Ct. 1237, 79 L.Ed.2d 552 (1984) (production of documents would "tacitly [concede] the existence of the papers demanded and their possession or control by the taxpayer. It also would indicate the taxpayer's belief that the papers are those described in the subpoena.").

9.   More on Incriminating Acts of Production

In *Braswell v. United States*, 487 U.S. 99, 108 S.Ct. 2284, 101 L.Ed.2d 98 (1988), the president of a company objected to a subpoena on the basis that the "act of producing the records would incriminate him in violation of his Fifth Amendment privilege against self-incrimination." The Court held that, whether a "subpoena is addressed to the corporation, or as here, to the individual in his capacity as a custodian, a corporate custodian such as petitioner may not resist a subpoena for corporate records on Fifth Amendment grounds. [T]he custodian's act of production is not deemed a personal act, but rather an act of the corporation. Any claim of Fifth Amendment privilege asserted by the agent would be tantamount to a claim of privilege by the corporation—which of course possesses no such privilege. . . . [I]n a criminal prosecution against the custodian, the Government may not introduce into evidence before the jury the fact that the subpoena was served upon and the corporation's documents were delivered by one particular individual, the custodian. The Government has the right, however, to use the corporation's act of production against the custodian. The Government may offer testimony—for example, from the process server who delivered the subpoena and from the individual who received the records—establishing that the corporation produced the records subpoenaed. The jury may draw from the corporation's act of production the conclusion that the records in question are authentic corporate records, which the corporation possessed, and which it produced in response to the subpoena."

G. PARALLEL PROCEEDINGS

In some instances, when the government seeks information from companies or private individuals, it is pursuing both civil and criminal objectives. If the government is contemplating criminal charges, a potential defendant might object that it is inappropriate for the agency to use its civil powers to gather information as a predicate to a criminal prosecution.

1. *Dresser Industries* & Parallel Proceedings

In *Securities and Exchange Commission v. Dresser Industries, Inc.*, 628 F.2d 1368 (D.C.Cir.1980), Dresser Industries sought protection because it claimed that the SEC was conducting parallel civil and criminal investigations. The court rejected the challenge holding that, in "the absence of substantial prejudice to the rights of the parties involved, such parallel proceedings are unobjectionable under our jurisprudence." As a result, as a general rule, courts should not grant a stay. However, "a court may decide in its discretion to stay civil proceedings, postpone civil discovery, or impose protective orders and conditions 'when the interests of justice seem to require such action, sometimes at the request of the prosecution, [sometimes] at the request of the defense[.]' The court must make such determinations in the light of the particular circumstances of the case." The court held that a stay might be required when "there is specific evidence of agency bad faith or malicious governmental tactics," so that civil proceedings might be deferred until criminal proceedings are complete.

2. United States v. Kordel

In *United States v. Kordel*, 397 U.S. 1, 90 S.Ct. 763, 25 L.Ed.2d 1 (1970), after the government used interrogatories against a corporation in a civil proceeding, plaintiffs claimed a violation of their Fifth Amendment privilege against compulsory self-incrimination when the interrogatory answers were used against them in a criminal proceeding. The Court rejected the claim noting that individuals who were concerned about incriminating themselves could refuse to testify in the civil proceeding based on their Fifth Amendment privilege against compulsory self-incrimination. The difficulty is that a corporation does not have a privilege against self-incrimination, and can be required to appoint an agent who can testify without fear of incrimination. Only when no company representative can answer the interrogatories might it be appropriate to stay the civil proceeding. The Court also held that it might take action if the government had "brought a civil action solely to obtain evidence for its criminal prosecution or has failed to advise the defendant in its civil proceeding that it contemplates his criminal prosecution."

3. *LaSalle National Bank* & "Good Faith"

In *United States v. LaSalle National Bank*, 437 U.S. 298, 98 S.Ct. 2357, 57 L.Ed.2d 221 (1978), as part of a broad-based investigation of an individual, the Internal Revenue Service (IRS) subpoenaed records from a bank. The subpoena was challenged on the basis that the IRS was involved in a criminal investigation, and that it was improperly using a civil investigation to gather information for a criminal prosecution. Recognizing that the IRS code contains interrelated criminal and civil elements, and that the civil and criminal proceedings separate only when the IRS recommends a criminal prosecution to the Department of Justice, the Court held that the IRS could not issue a subpoena for *solely* criminal purposes. A subpoena will be upheld if two requirements are met: "First, the summons must be issued before the Service recommends to the Department of Justice that a criminal prosecution, which reasonably would relate to the subject matter of the summons, be undertaken. Second, the Service at all times must use the summons authority in good-faith pursuit of the congressionally authorized purposes of § 7602."

TRUE–FALSE QUESTIONS

1. Administrative searches are treated differently than police searches because they are not subject to the Fourth Amendment's warrant requirement.

2. In the administrative context, the concept of "probable cause" is defined differently than it is defined in the criminal law context.

3. For purposes of the Fourth Amendment, "closely regulated businesses" are treated differently than other businesses.

4. Businesses subject to the Occupational Safety and Health Act qualify as "closely regulated businesses."

5. The Fifth Amendment privilege against self-incrimination protects not only individuals, but also corporations and unincorporated associations.

6. A person may resist compliance with a subpoena to produce documents (subpoena *duces tecum*) based on the privilege against self-incrimination.

7. Administrative agencies are flatly prohibited from conducting parallel civil and criminal proceedings.

8. The Fourth Amendment prohibits administrative subpoenas.

9. Administrative subpoenas can suffer from too much indefiniteness or breadth and therefore must "particularly describe" the documents to be produced.

10. A company may refuse to produce documents if the corporate custodian cannot produce them without incriminating him/herself.

MULTIPLE CHOICE QUESTIONS

1. Which of the following businesses do *not* qualify as "closely regulated businesses."

    A. Liquor Stores;

    B. Fire arms dealers;

    C. Automobile junkyards;

    D. Automobile factories.

2. Which of the following objections may be validly raised against an administrative subpoena:

    A. That the subpoena constitutes an "unreasonable search and seizure" in violation of the Fourth Amendment.

    B. That the subpoena does not particularly describe the documents to be produced.

    C. That compliance with the subpoena would violate the producer's privilege against self-incrimination.

    D. All of the above.

3. In *Braswell v. United States*, the Court articulated which of the following propositions:

    A. When a subpoena is addressed to a corporation, the corporate custodian (who the documents would incriminate) cannot refuse to produce them on Fifth Amendment grounds.

    B. In a criminal prosecution against the custodian of records, the Government may not introduce into evidence the fact that the corporation's documents were delivered by one particular individual, the custodian.

C.   The Government has the right to use the corporation's act of production against the custodian. The Government may offer testimony—for example, from the process server who delivered the subpoena and from the individual who received the records—establishing that the corporation produced the records subpoenaed

D.   All of the above.

ESSAY QUESTIONS

1.   You represent a veterinarian who has x-ray equipment. Because the equipment uses radiation, it is periodically subject to inspection. Suppose that a radiation inspector shows up at your client's office without a warrant and asks for permission to inspect the x-ray equipment. Your client has called you for advice. How would you advise the client.

2.   Suppose that you represent a company which is subject to a civil proceeding brought before the United States Department of Energy (DOE). However, you fear that DOE, in conjunction with the Justice Department is strongly considering a criminal prosecution based on the same facts. DOE serves an administrative subpoena on your client demanding that your corporate custodian, John James, produce and testify regarding company documents. There is a significant likelihood that the documents will incriminate both James and the corporation. What actions should you, as corporate counsel, take?

3.   Your client has been engaged in illegal bookmaking operations and has substantial illicit income. At income tax time, he is aware of his obligation to file a federal tax return. However, he is also aware that, if he declares his illegal bookmaking income, he will be prosecuted for bookmaking. Under these circumstances, how would you advise your client to proceed?

ANSWERS TO TRUE–FALSE QUESTIONS

1.   False.   In fact, administrative searches are not treated differently than police searches. Both are subject to the Fourth Amendment's warrant requirement except that the concept of probable cause is defined differently in the administrative context.

2.   True.   In the administrative context, the concept of "probable cause" is defined differently than it is defined in the criminal law context.

Instead of requiring "particularized" evidence against the business or place to be searched, the Court requires only "reasonable administrative standards." To inspect for blight, probable cause can be based on the fact that the area is blighted. It matters not that the house or business to be inspected does not suffer from blight.

3. True. For purposes of the Fourth Amendment, "closely regulated businesses" are treated differently than other businesses. The major difference is that they are not subject to the warrant requirement and probable cause is not a prerequisite to a search.

4. False. The Court has explicitly rejected the idea that businesses subject to the Occupational Safety and Health Act qualify as "closely regulated businesses."

5. False. The Fifth Amendment privilege against self-incrimination protects only individuals, and does not protect corporations and unincorporated associations.

6. False. A person may not resist compliance with a subpoena to produce documents (subpoena *duces tecum*) based on the privilege against self-incrimination. The privilege protects only against compelled "testimonial" incrimination and does not protect against the production of documents.

7. False. Administrative agencies are not "flatly" prohibited from conducting parallel civil and criminal proceedings. On the contrary, as a general rule, parallel proceedings are permitted except in limited situations.

8. False. The Fourth Amendment does not prohibit administrative subpoenas.

9. True. Administrative subpoenas can suffer from too much indefiniteness or breadth and therefore must "particularly describe" the documents to be produced.

10. False. If the corporate custodian cannot produce company documents without incriminating him/herself, the company is required to designate someone else to make the production.

ANSWERS TO MULTIPLE CHOICE QUESTIONS

1. Answer (D) is correct. Answer (A) is incorrect because the Court has treated liquor stores as a "closely regulated business." Answer (B) (fire arms dealers)

and Answer (C) (automobile junkyards) are both incorrect because the Court has also treated these businesses as "closely regulated businesses." Answer (D) is correct because automobile factories have not been treated as closely regulated.

2. Answer (B) is correct. Answer (A) is incorrect because the Court has not held that the Fourth Amendment prohibits administrative subpoenas as "unreasonable searches and seizures." Answer (B) is correct because the Court has held that subpoenas must particularly describe the documents to be produced. Answer (C) is incorrect because compliance with a subpoena will rarely violate the producer's privilege against self-incrimination. Answer (D), "all of the above" are correct, is incorrect because both Answer (A) and Answer (C) are incorrect.

3. Answer (D), "all of the above," is correct. As a result, Answer (A) is correct in asserting that *Braswell v. United States* held that, when a subpoena is addressed to a corporation, the corporate custodian (who the documents would incriminate) cannot refuse to produce them on Fifth Amendment grounds. Answer (B) is also correct because *Braswell* held that, in a criminal prosecution against the custodian, the Government may not introduce into evidence the fact that the corporation's documents were delivered by one particular individual, the custodian. Finally, and likewise, Answer (C) is correct because *Braswell* held that the Government has the right, however, to use the corporation's act of production against the custodian. The Government may offer testimony—for example, from the process server who delivered the subpoena and from the individual who received the records—establishing that the corporation produced the records subpoenaed.

ANSWERS TO ESSAY QUESTIONS

1. The simple answer is that the client should probably permit the inspector to examine the equipment for radiation leaks. Under the Fourth Amendment, since the inspection qualifies as a "search," the inspection is subject to the prohibition against "unreasonable searches and seizures." In *Camara*, the Court held that such inspections require a warrant. As a result, the client has the right to refuse the inspector's request and force the inspector to obtain a warrant in order to conduct the inspection. However, unless the client is aware of a serious violation which could result in very serious penalties, the client is probably better off to consent to the inspection. If consent is refused, the inspector is likely to obtain a warrant and to return in a foul humor intent on finding a violation.

2. Although there is very little chance of success, you might move to stay the administrative proceeding pending the outcome of potential criminal proceedings. If the request is denied, the company probably has little choice but to produce the documents. However, as corporate attorney, you have an ethical obligation to advise James that he may incriminate himself if he chooses to testify, and you should advise him to retain independent counsel to represent himself. If he decides not to testify, you should appoint someone else to produce the documents.

3. This situation presents your client with a dilemma. Obviously, if the client files a false tax return, and the return would be false if the client failed to declare his bookmaking income, he can be prosecuted for filing a fraudulent tax return. On the other hand, if the client fails to file a return, he can be prosecuted for that failure. The accepted wisdom is that the client should file the return, but assert his privilege against self-incrimination on the return itself. Of course, if the client adopts that course of action, the return would undoubtedly start an Internal Revenue Service criminal investigation which could result in evidence of illegal bookmaking and a subsequent prosecution. So, undoubtedly, the client will opt either to file a false return or to not file. Ethically, as a lawyer, you can not advise the client to take either course of action.

CHAPTER SIX

Agency Structure

A. INTRODUCTION

Administrative agencies raise basic questions about their power and their control by the political branches. In particular, questions arise about Congress's authority to delegate legislative power to the agency and its power to authorize agency courts to adjudicate disputes. In addition, issues arise about the ability of Congress and the President to control agencies. This chapter takes up these topics in that order.

B. NON–DELEGATION

1. General Rule

The non-delegation doctrine derives from Article I's statement that "all legislative powers" granted to the federal government were to be vested in Congress. From this grew the idea that, as the People had allocated this power to Congress, it could not be delegated to other entities, such as administrative agencies.

2. History

From the beginning of the Constitution it was recognized that agencies would have to make some decisions. Throughout the 19th and early 20th centuries, the Supreme Court experimented with formulas to allow agency decision-making consistent with the non-delegation principle. For example, in the early 19th century Chief Justice Marshall spoke of agencies simply finding the facts that triggered the policy choices made by Congress. In the 1911 case of *United States v. Grimaud*, 220 U.S. 506, 31 S.Ct. 480, 55 L.Ed. 563 (1911), the Court spoke of the agency simply "filling in the details" of a statutory scheme.

3.   Modern Rule

The modern rule, from *J.W. Hampton v. United States*, 276 U.S. 394, 48 S.Ct. 348, 72 L.Ed. 624 (1928), is that Congress must lay down an "intelligible principle" to guide the agency's action.

4.   New Deal Statutes Failing the "Intelligible Principle" Test

The Supreme Court has invalidated statutes on non-delegation grounds only twice, both in 1935. In *Panama Refining Co. v. Ryan*, 293 U.S. 388, 55 S.Ct. 241, 79 L.Ed. 446 (1935) the Court struck down a statute authorizing the President to ban the interstate shipment of certain oil, concluding that the statute did not provide guidance as to the conditions under which the President should exercise his authority. Similarly, in *A.L.A. Schechter Poultry Corp. v. United States*, 295 U.S. 495, 55 S.Ct. 837, 79 L.Ed. 1570 (1935) the Court found that the National Industrial Recovery Act both granted the President near-complete power over interstate commerce and furnished no standards under which he was to exercise this extraordinarily broad power.

5.   Post New–Deal History of the Non–Delegation Doctrine

Since 1935 the Supreme Court has never struck a statute down on non-delegation grounds. The Court has upheld, among others, delegations to agencies to regulate a particular industry "in the public interest," and to set "just and reasonable" rates for interstate shipping of goods. In some cases the Court has read statutes narrowly, so as to avoid reaching the question whether Congress violated the doctrine, using the basic principle that statutes should be construed so as to avoid constitutional questions.

6.   Rejection of Agency Cures for Non–Delegation Flaws

In *Whitman v. American Trucking Assn.*, 531 U.S. 457, 121 S.Ct. 903, 149 L.Ed.2d 1 (2001) the Court rejected a non-delegation challenge to the Clean Air Act's requirement that the agency regulate air pollution by imposing standards "requisite to protect public health" with "an adequate margin of safety." In the lower court's view, the agency itself could set standards that would limit its own discretion, thus curing any non-delegation problem. The Supreme Court in *American Trucking* rejected that approach, concluding that the doctrine required that the statute itself, rather than subsequent agency action, contain the requisite intelligible principle.

C.   ADJUDICATION BY NON–ARTICLE III COURTS

Another type of delegation occurs when Congress provides that agencies, rather than Article III courts, should adjudicate cases arising under the statutes the agency administers. These situations raise an issue analogous to the non-delegation doctrine, because of the language of Article III that states that "the judicial power of the United States" shall be vested in the Supreme Court and whatever inferior federal courts Congress creates.

1. Agency Courts Are Not Article III Courts

Agency courts are not Article III courts. Judges in agency courts ("administrative law judges" or "ALJs") are not selected with the advice and consent of the Senate, and they do not enjoy the salary and tenure protections enjoyed by Article III judges.

2. Early Doctrine: The Public/Private Right Distinction

In *Murray's Lessee v. Hoboken Land Imp. Co.*, 59 U.S. 272, 18 How. 272, 15 L.Ed. 372 (1855), the Supreme Court distinguished between public and private rights when determining when Congress could place the adjudication of federal law cases in a non-Article III tribunal. Public rights were defined as rights between the government and private parties, while private rights were rights as between private parties. According to the Court, since Congress created public rights, it could place their adjudication in non-Article III courts if it wished. Private rights, however, had to be litigated in Article III courts.

3. Further Refinement: *Crowell v. Benson* and "Constitutional" Facts

In *Crowell v. Benson*, 285 U.S. 22, 52 S.Ct. 285, 76 L.Ed. 598 (1932), the Court further elaborated on the conditions under which Congress could place the adjudication of rights in a non-Article III court. In *Crowell* the Court was faced with the issue whether an agency court could engage in fact-finding in the course of adjudicating a claim. The Court held that, with regard to "constitutional" facts (*i.e.*, facts on which constitutional rights depended, or facts which determined whether the federal government had regulatory authority, e.g., whether a transaction took place in interstate commerce), the Article III court had the duty, not just to review the agency court's fact findings *de novo*, but to develop the facts from scratch, e.g., by taking evidence.

4. *Northern Pipeline* and *Union Carbide*

In *Northern Pipeline Const. Co. v. Marathon Pipe Line Co.*, 458 U.S. 50, 102 S.Ct. 2858, 73 L.Ed.2d 598 (1982), the Court struck down the structure of bankruptcy courts Congress had established. Congress established bankruptcy courts as non-Article III courts, with the power to hear any claims dealing with a party that was in bankruptcy proceedings. There was no majority opinion in *Northern Pipeline*; however, the plurality opinion continued to apply the public/private rights distinction from *Murray's Lessee*. Three years later, in *Thomas v. Union Carbide Agr. Products*, 473 U.S. 568, 105 S.Ct. 3325, 87

L.Ed.2d 409 (1985), a Court majority backtracked from *Northern Pipeline*'s insistence on that distinction, stating that Congress "may create a seemingly 'private' right that is so closely integrated into a public regulatory scheme as to be a matter appropriate" for adjudication by an agency.

5. The Modern Rule: Balancing

In *Commodity Futures Trading Com'n v. Schor*, 478 U.S. 833, 106 S.Ct. 3245, 92 L.Ed.2d 675 (1986), the Court enunciated a balancing test for deciding the agency court issue. In *Schor* the Court considered a complex scheme where a customer of a commodities broker could bring a statutorily-created "reparations" claim against the broker in an agency court, and the broker could bring a common law contract counterclaim against the customer in the same agency court. The customer objected to this latter claim being heard by an agency court.

a. Public/Private Rights

In the *Schor* test, the nature of the right as public or private remained relevant, but only as one factor for the court to consider. Because the counterclaim was clearly a private right—it existed between two private parties, and was based on the common law—this factor cut against the constitutionality of the agency court's authority to adjudicate the claim.

b. The Essential Attributes of Judicial Power

The next factor considered whether the essential attributes of the Article III judicial power remained with Article III courts. Here, the Court noted that Article III courts reviewed the agency court's legal conclusions *de novo*, and the agency court's orders under a "weight of the evidence" standard, both of which adequately safeguarded the role of Article III courts.

c. The Powers of the Agency Court

The Court also noted that the agency court did not exercise many of the powers normally exercised by Article III courts. For example, it did not have the power to preside over trials, issue writs of habeas corpus, or enforce its own orders. Moreover, the jurisdiction of the agency court was limited only to counterclaims growing out of commodities transactions, a small part of the regular business of Article III courts, and far from the general federal question jurisdiction enjoyed by federal trial courts.

d. Congress's Motivations

Finally, *Schor* noted that Congress did not create the agency courts in that case in order to aggrandize power to itself, or otherwise to reduce the power of Article III courts. Rather, it created these courts in order to provide an efficient dispute resolution mechanism, able to hear not just the customer's reparations claim, but any counterclaims that might grow out of the same business transaction.

6. A Return to the Public/Private Rights Distinction

In *Stern v. Marshall*, ___ U.S. ___, 131 S.Ct. 2594, 180 L.Ed.2d 475 (2011), the Court re-emphasized the public/private rights distinction when deciding when the Constitution required an Article III judge to decide a case. *Stern*, like *Northern Pipeline*, dealt with a bankruptcy court adjudicating a complex bankruptcy involving multiple claims and counterclaims. One of those counterclaims, on a common law cause of action, was alleged to be the type that had to be heard by an Article III court, rather than the non-Article III bankruptcy court. The Supreme Court agreed, concluding that that counterclaim involved a private right. At the same time, the Court said it was leaving *Schor* undisturbed, on the ground that *Schor* dealt with a situation where Congress had given the agency the power to engage in substantive regulation of a given field. By contrast, the bankruptcy court was simply an adjudicator of claims grounded in other sources of law, such as the common law.

7. Summary

The Court has not traveled a steady path in deciding the question of Congress's power to create agency courts. The recent *Stern* case, even though it explicitly distinguished rather than questioned *Schor*, raises new questions about the role of the public/private rights distinction and, by contrast, the other, more functional, factors *Schor* identified as relevant.

D. THE LEGISLATIVE VETO AND OTHER METHODS OF CONGRESSIONAL CONTROL

1. Introduction

When Congress delegates broad power to agencies it often wishes to retain some supervisory power over how the agency uses its discretion. Congress has a variety of tools by which it can perform this supervision.

2. The Legislative Veto Explained

One way Congress can supervise agencies is by enacting a subsequent statute restricting how the agency can use its discretion. But because this is a cumbersome process, in the early 20th century it began inserting provisions in statutes authorizing it to restrict agency action by means less than a full-blown statute. For example, these provisions might authorize restrictions on agency action if imposed by both houses of Congress (without presenting the proposal to the President for his signature or veto), by one house of Congress, or even by a committee of one house. All these types of provisions came to be known as "legislative vetoes."

3. The Legislative Veto Is Unconstitutional

In *Immigration and Naturalization Service v. Chadha*, 462 U.S. 919, 103 S.Ct. 2764, 77 L.Ed.2d 317 (1983), the Supreme Court struck down the legislative veto. It held that legislative vetoes were the equivalent of legislation, since they altered legal rights and duties. Because they were essentially legislation, the Court held that they had to go through the process of bicameralism and presentment provided in the Constitution for lawmaking.

4. "Laying" Process Still Constitutional

Chadha did not disturb other methods Congress has to oversee agency action. For example, Congress may still require that proposed agency action not take effect for a stated period of time, in order to give Congress the chance to review the action and determine if it wished to countermand it via a full-blown statute or some other mechanism.

5. Budget Constraints

Congress also retains the power to appropriate funds for agencies. This power allows it to exert some control over agency action; for example, Congress can specify that none of the money it is appropriating for an agency can be used to enforce a particular regulation. However, since budget appropriations must go through both houses and be presented to the President, they do not constitute legislative vetoes and thus are consistent with *Chadha*.

6. Confirmation Proceedings

Because agency heads must be confirmed by the Senate, confirmation proceedings present the Senate with the opportunity to review and express its opinions of particular agency initiatives, and to extract commitments from the nominee. Because these commitments are not formally legally binding, they are consistent with *Chadha*.

7. Informal Oversight

Finally, Congress retains informal oversight power. In particular, Congress has the authority to hold hearings and call bureaucrats to testify, to justify and explain their regulatory actions. As with discussions in confirmation hearings, these oversight activities themselves have no formal legal effect, however, and thus do not constitute legislative vetoes. Of course, they may lead Congress to enact a statute that does restrict the agency's discretion.

E. THE APPOINTMENT AND REMOVAL POWER

1. Introduction

One of the basic ways in which a President seeks to control agency action is by appointing as heads of agencies people who share his regulatory philosophy, and dismissing those who do not share it. Questions arise, though, over whether Congress can restrict the President's powers in this regard.

2. Appointments Power Is Provided in Article II

Article II gives the President the power to nominate "Ambassadors . . . and all other Officers of the United States," but then goes on to state that "Congress may by Law vest the Appointment of such inferior Officers, as they think proper, in the President alone, in the Courts of Law, or in the Heads of Departments." This language has led to the distinction between "principal" and "inferior" officers.

3. Principal/Inferior Officer Distinction Based on Supervision and Scope of Duties

In *Morrison v. Olson*, 487 U.S. 654, 108 S.Ct. 2597, 101 L.Ed.2d 569 (1988) the Supreme Court determined that Special Prosecutors established under the now-defunct Special Prosecutor statute were inferior officers, and thus could be appointed by a panel of judges, rather than the President. The Court noted the prosecutor's limited jurisdiction, the fact he was supervised by another officer (the Attorney General), and the fact that the prosecutor's office terminated upon conclusion of the investigation it was charged with pursuing.

4. Cabinet Level Officers and Agency Heads are "Principal" Officers

Based on this analysis, cabinet level officers and heads of agencies are principal officers, which must be appointed by the President and confirmed by the Senate. Some sub-cabinet officers also fall into this category, although application of the *Morrison* criteria suggests that these decisions must be made on a case-by-case basis.

5. History of the Removal Power

In *Myers v. United States*, 272 U.S. 52, 47 S.Ct. 21, 71 L.Ed. 160 (1926), the Court enunciated a very broad presidential removal power, stating that the

President needed to have confidence in his subordinates if he was to carry out his constitutionally-assigned functions. In *Humphrey's Executor v. United States*, 295 U.S. 602, 55 S.Ct. 869, 79 L.Ed. 1611 (1935), the Court modified this formula slightly, allowing Congress to restrict the President's removal power if the officer was not performing an "executive function."

6. The Removal Power in *Morrison*

In *Morrison v. Olson* the Court stated that the President had the constitutional authority to remove an officer only if denial of that power would make it impossible for him to carry out his constitutionally-prescribed duties.

7. Nature of the Officer's Duties Still Relevant

The *Morrison* Court stated that the nature of the official's function as executive or not remained relevant to that determination. However, it disapproved of the idea that the removal power turned solely on the nature of the officer's duties.

8. Retention of Control by the Executive Branch

In *Morrison* the Court noted that the Attorney General retained some control over the Special Prosecutor, via a provision that allowed the Attorney General to remove the prosecutor for "good cause."

9. No Legal Obligation to Appoint the Special Prosecutor

The court also noted that under the terms of the statute, the Attorney General did not have to appoint a special prosecutor if he found, based on an initial investigation, that there were no grounds to believe that illegalities occurred.

10. No Congressional Aggrandizement

It also noted that there was no indication that Congress was attempting to aggrandize itself. Congress placed appointment and termination of the prosecutor with a panel of judges, not with Congress itself.

11. *Morrison* Restricts Presidential Removal Power

Because *Morrison* upheld restrictions on the President's power to remove a criminal prosecutor, which is at the heart of the presidential power to enforce laws, it is clear that *Morrison* made it easier for Congress to restrict the President's power to remove officers at will.

12. *Free Enterprise Fund*

In *Free Enterprise Fund v. Public Company Accounting Oversight Board*, ___ U.S. ___, 130 S.Ct. 3138, 177 L.Ed.2d 706 (2010), the Court imposed a limit on congressional attempts to restrict direct presidential control over agency officials. In *Free Enterprise Fund* the Court found unconstitutional an administrative structure in which particular officials (the heads of the Public Company Accounting Oversight Board, or "PCAOB") were removable only for good cause by the commissioners of the Securities and Exchange Commission, who were themselves removable by the President only for good cause. The Court held that this double insulation from direct presidential removal authority unconstitutionally removed too much presidential control from the PCAOB. It noted that in *Morrison* only one level of good-cause protection existed between the Special Prosecutor and the President, given that the Attorney General was removable at will by the President. Thus, while *Morrison* remains good law, it appears as though the Court has drawn a line limiting more aggressive congressional attempts to insulate officials from at-will presidential removal.

TRUE–FALSE QUESTIONS

1. The nature of the right being adjudicated is irrelevant to modern doctrine about the authority of agency courts to adjudicate federal law claims.

2. A statutory provision that both houses may overturn an agency regulation if they so agree by a 2/3 margin—the amount needed to override a presidential veto—remains constitutional even after *INS v. Chadha*.

3. The intent of Congress is irrelevant when considering the constitutionality of an agency adjudication scheme.

4. The constitutional authority of a President to appoint officers turns in large part on whether the officer is classified as an inferior officer.

5. Once Congress delegates power to an administrative agency it is unable to exert control over how it uses its discretion, except by the informal mechanisms of confirmation hearings and other informal oversight.

6. Congress may vest the appointment of inferior officers anywhere, including itself, the courts or the President.

7. The Court has wielded the non-delegation power aggressively to police overbroad delegations of power to the agencies.

8. As long as the Court finds Congress to have stated an "intelligible principle" in a statute, the non-delegation requirement is satisfied.

MULTIPLE CHOICE QUESTION

Which would be the most constitutionally questionable feature of a statute limiting the President's power to remove a particular inferior officer?

A. A provision limiting the President's ability to fire to situations where he finds "good cause" to do so.

B. A provision requiring Congress to approve of any removal decision.

C. A provision giving a federal judge the power to remove the officer.

D. A provision authorizing the President to fire the officer when the President deems the officer's policies to conflict with those of the President himself.

ESSAY QUESTION

In order to combat identify theft on the Internet, Congress enacts a statute regulating the use of private information obtained from the Internet, and places adjudication of claims alleging misuse of that information in courts set up inside the Federal Trade Commission (FTC). The statute states that Congress is creating this adjudicative scheme in order "to provide a convenient and simple method to help consumers who have been victimized by misuse of private information obtained by Internet retailers." Under the scheme any person can sue any other person who allegedly has violated the statute. The agency court has the power to enforce its own orders, and its jurisdiction is limited to cases arising under the statute as well as to common law counterclaims arising out of the same transaction as the one giving rise to the statutory claim. It has the power to decide questions of law and questions of fact, both of which are subject to *de novo* review on appeal to a federal court.

Smith sues Jones.com, an Internet marketer, for violating his rights under the statute. Jones.com counterclaims that Smith violated the contract he agreed to when he bought merchandise on the Jones.com site. Can the Jones.com counterclaim be adjudicated in the agency court?

ANSWERS TO TRUE–FALSE QUESTIONS

1. False.   Under the *Schor* balancing test and *Stern*, the nature of the right remains relevant—indeed, in *Stern* it was dispositive.

2. False.   *Chadha* requires presentment to the President, and this requirement is not obviated by a requirement that the congressional action be by

a sufficient majority to override a presidential veto.

3. False. Under *Schor*'s balancing test, a concern that Congress was attempting to aggrandize power for itself would militate against the agency adjudication scheme being constitutional.

4. True. Article II states that inferior officers need not be appointed by the President; rather, Congress can vest their appointment in agency heads, the President or the courts.

5. False. Even after *Chadha* Congress may enact a statute limiting the agency's discretion or preventing it from using any appropriated funds to act in a certain way.

6. False. The Appointments clause allows the vesting of the inferior officer appointment power in the heads of agencies, the courts or the President, but not in Congress itself.

7. False. In all its history the Court has only struck down two statutes as violating the non-delegation doctrine, and has not done so since 1935.

8. True. The "intelligible principle" standard was enunciated in 1928, and remains the rule today.

ANSWER TO MULTIPLE CHOICE QUESTION

The correct answer is (B). In *Morrison v. Olson* the Court allowed more restrictions on the President's power to remove an officer than it had before. In particular, it approved of a provision requiring the President to make a finding of good cause before firing the officer, and approved of a provision giving a panel of federal judges the power to terminate the office of the Special Prosecutor. This makes answer choices (A) and (C) constitutional, and thus incorrect answers to the question. Answer choice (B) is the correct answer, because in *Morrison* the Court expressed concern about any removal provision that would seem to aggrandize Congress's own power, such as one giving it a role in the removal decision. Moreover, such a provision would be problematic as the Appointments Clause authorizes Congress to vest the appointment (and thus, by implication, the removal) of inferior officers in several institutions, but not including Congress. Answer choice (D) is incorrect because there is nothing constitutionally problematic in Congress giving the President a broad removal power; the only question is whether such a broad removal power is constitutionally required.

ANSWER TO ESSAY QUESTION

The right asserted by Jones.com is clearly a private law right, as it runs between two private parties, and is based on the common law. This fact would militate against the agency court's power to hear the case. On the other hand the fact that the agency court's jurisdiction to hear common law claims is limited to those claims arising out of the statutory claims probably militates in favor of constitutionality. It makes sense that Congress might wish to have all claims arising out of a single transaction heard in one forum. Finally, it appears as though Congress had a good reason for placing adjudication of these claims in an agency court—in particular, it does not appear as though Congress was trying to aggrandize power to itself.

Militating against the agency court's authority is the fact that the agency court has the power to enforce its own orders; the Court in *Schor* noted this power as one of the essential attributes of the Article III judicial power. On the other hand, the agency court has only limited jurisdiction, and its legal and factual conclusions receive no deference from the federal court reviewing its decisions. This is a close call, but on balance there's a good chance a court would uphold this scheme.

CHAPTER SEVEN

Public Access to Agency Processes

A. THE NEED FOR GOVERNMENT OPENNESS

For many years, government operations and government documents were largely shielded from public viewing and disclosure. There were exceptions to this rule. For example, Article I, Section 4, clause 3, provides that each house of Congress shall keep and publish from time to time a journal of its proceedings, which must include a record of any Presidential vetoes and "the names of the persons voting for and against" bills in the houses. Article I, Section 9, clause 7 mandates a "public accounting" of receipts and expenditures of the United States. But the inner workings of most administrative agencies were secret. Eventually, a movement started to encourage greater governmental openness. This movement was prompted by the notion that, in a democracy, where citizens are expected to cast informed votes for candidates and on issues, greater governmental disclosure is both necessary and desirable.

B. THE NEED FOR GOVERNMENTAL SECRECY

Despite the move for openness, commentators have recognized that some governmental processes must be kept confidential, including matters related to foreign affairs and national security. In addition, as the United States Supreme Court recognized in *United States v. Nixon*, 418 U.S. 683, 94 S.Ct. 3090, 41 L.Ed.2d 1039 (1974), a President's communications with his advisers are protected by the so-called Executive Privilege. In the presidential context, the Court concluded that confidentiality is "fundamental to the operation of Government and inextricably rooted in the separation of powers under the Constitution."

C. HISTORY OF ADMINISTRATIVE SECRECY

Despite the need to protect some communications, many felt that administrative agencies have historically been too secretive. Agencies were generally not required to disclose information related to their internal workings or even their rules and regulations, and many refused to do so. Indeed, in 1935 a government lawyer discovered soon before arguing a case before the Supreme Court that a previously-unknown executive order had undermined the foundation for the regulation the lawyer was defending. This incident led to the enactment of the law establishing the *Federal Register* as the source for official regulatory actions.

D. THE APA'S DISCLOSURE PROVISIONS

The APA shifted the paradigm somewhat by forcing agencies to publish and make available various types of information. In addition to requiring disclosure of agency organization and procedures, it also required disclosure of an agency's substantive rules, statements of general policy or interpretations adopted for the guidance of the public, and final opinions and orders.

E. THE FREEDOM OF INFORMATION ACT

In 1966, Congress passed the Freedom of Information Act, which created a right of access to government information.

1. FOIA Is a Disclosure Statute

FOIA, section 552(a)(3), is widely regarded as a "disclosure" statute. In other words, it generally requires agencies to disclose information: "upon any request for records which reasonably describes such records and is made in accordance with published rules stating the time, place, fees (if any), and procedures to be followed," the agency must "make the records promptly available to any person."

2. FOIA Requests

FOIA requests may be made by "any person," including foreign citizens, corporations, and governments. *See Stone v. Export–Import Bank of the U.S.*, 552 F.2d 132 (5th Cir. 1977). The person seeking the records need not show any need or justification for making the request.

a. Reasonable Description

In order to invoke FOIA, the individual who requests documents must "reasonably describe" the records being sought. The description must be such that "a professional employee of the agency who was familiar with the subject area of the request [would be able] to locate the record with a reasonable amount of effort." If a request is too broad and burdensome, the agency may refuse to comply. *See Keese v. United States*, 632 F.Supp. 85 (S.D. Tex. 1985) (request not reasonably specific).

b. Agency Rules and Regulations

FOIA requires agencies to create rules and regulations governing FOIA requests. Specifically, agencies may prescribe where and how to make FOIA requests, and may also establish rules governing fees, fee waivers, and pre-payment requirements. FOIA also requires requests to be made in accordance with any published agency rules.

c. "Agency Records"

FOIA only requires agencies to produce "agency records." Under FOIA, the term "agency" is broadly defined to include, not only traditional governmental agencies, but also governmental corporations and the Executive Office of the President. Swept in by these definitions are the President and his staff, the Office of Management and Budget (OMB), the Office of Science and Technology (OST), and the Council on Environmental Quality (CEQ). Left out of the definition is the Council of Economic Advisors. The term "agency records" includes records in the "possession" of a covered agency.

3. FOIA Exemptions

Consistent with the idea that some governmental information must be protected against disclosure, FOIA provides that nine different types of material are exempt from disclosure. The exemptions are: classified information; internal agency personnel rules and practices; information specifically exempted from disclosure by statute; private commercial or trade secret information; inter-agency or intra-agency privileged communications; personnel, medical, or similar files the disclosure of which would constitute a clearly unwarranted invasion of privacy; information compiled for law enforcement purposes; information related to reports for or by an agency involved in regulating financial institutions; and geological information concerning wells.

a. Redaction of Exempt Material

When a requested document contains both exempt and non-exempt material, the agency is required to disclose "reasonably segregable portions" of the document. Portions of a document are deemed to be "reasonably segregable" if they would be intelligible if segregated. In considering whether to order disclosure, courts will take into account the level of burden that would be imposed if segregation were required.

b. FOIA Indices

When an agency claims that particular documents are exempt from disclosure, the requester needs some disclosure in order to challenge the exemption claim. Because of the exempt nature, the agency will generally refuse to allow the requester to examine the documents. Courts will require agencies to prepare a *"Vaughn* Index" of withheld records. *See Vaughn v. Rosen*, 484 F.2d 820 (D.C. Cir. 1973). The index must describe each document, or withheld portion of the document, and provide an explanation for the agency's decision to withhold. This explanation must include an explanation of the reasons why the document was withheld, specifying applicable exemptions. Using the *Vaughn* index, the requester has some information on which to challenge the exemption claim.

c. Classified Information

The exemption for "classified information" is designed to protect national security information, including documents marked "Top Secret," "Secret," or "Confidential" pursuant to executive order. FOIA does not allow courts to delve into the broader question of whether a classification order is valid, but it does allow a court to consider whether a document has been properly classified under the order. In a few cases, where the agency refuses to identify a document on the basis that the mere acknowledgment of the document's existence would impair national security, the agency need not acknowledge the document's existence. *See Phillippi v. CIA*, 546 F.2d 1009 (D.C. Cir. 1976). Courts are usually deferential to claims that documents fit within this exemption.

d. Internal Personnel Rules

FOIA's second exemption (for "internal agency personnel rules and practices") is not so strictly enforced. In *Crooker v. BATF*, 670 F.2d 1051 (D.C. Cir. 1981) *(en banc)*, the court held that a BATF training manual containing agency surveillance techniques was exempt from disclosure. Basically, courts have distinguished between documents containing information that would interfere with proper agency functioning and those that would not. The former are exempt from disclosure.

e. Specifically Exempted by Statute

Various federal statutes protect and exempt governmental information. However, the Court has made it clear that Congress must be clear about its decision to "specifically exempt" particular types of information in order to invoke this exemption. *Administrator, FAA v. Robertson*, 422 U.S. 255, 95 S.Ct. 2140, 45 L.Ed.2d 164 (1975).

f. Confidential Business Information

FOIA also exempts trade secrets and commercial or financial information obtained from persons that is privileged or confidential under the Constitution, a statute, or the common law. In *Critical Mass Energy Project v. Nuclear Regulatory Commission*, 975 F.2d 871 (D.C. Cir. 1992) (*en banc*), the court held that information qualifies under this exemption if disclosure would "(1) . . . impair the Government's ability to obtain necessary information in the future; or (2) . . . cause substantial harm to the competitive position of the person from whom the information was obtained." However, the test has been qualified by the requirement that the information be such that the "provider would not customarily make available to the public."

g. Inter–or Intra–Agency Memoranda

FOIA also exempts inter-agency or intra-agency memoranda and letters "which would not be available by law to a party other than an agency in litigation with the agency."

(1) Scope of the Exemption

In general, this exemption protects documents that would have been protected under common law litigation privileges including executive privilege, attorney work-product privilege, attorney-client privilege confidential communications privilege, confidential commercial information of the government itself, and factual statements provided to air crash investigators.

(2) Executive Privilege & *Nixon*

United States v. Nixon, 418 U.S. 683, 94 S.Ct. 3090, 41 L.Ed.2d 1039 (1974), is the most famous application of executive privilege and the deliberative process privileges. These privileges are designed to ensure that the President and other high-level governmental officials receive "open and frank advice" from subordinates. The fear is that, if such advice were subject to disclosure, subordinates would be reluctant to speak candidly. Factual information does not qualify under the privilege.

h. Personal Privacy Documents

FOIA also protects "personnel and medical files and similar files the disclosure of which would constitute a clearly unwarranted invasion of privacy." Whether disclosure of a document would constitute a "clearly unwarranted invasion of privacy" requires consideration of the public interest in disclosure and the private interest in confidentiality. The more private the information, the more likely it is to be protected. However, this exemption is limited to natural persons, and does not include corporations or associations, and does not include individuals who have died. See, e.g., *FCC v. AT&T*, ___ U.S. ___, 131 S.Ct. 1177, 179 L.Ed.2d 132 (2011) (holding that the personal privacy exemption does not apply to corporations).

i. Law Enforcement Records

FOIA originally exempted "investigatory files compiled for law enforcement purposes," protecting even very old investigatory files. Congress later amended the exemption to protect investigatory files only if disclosure would "interfere with enforcement proceedings, deprive a person of a fair trial, constitute an unwarranted invasion of privacy, disclose the identity of a confidential source, disclose confidential investigative techniques and procedures, or endanger the life or safety of law enforcement personnel." For law enforcement or national security investigations there was an irrebuttable presumption that confidential information supplied solely by a confidential source would disclose the source's identity.

(1) 1986 Amendments

In 1986, Congress again amended the law enforcement exemption in several respects by eliminating the requirement that the records be "investigatory," requiring that the specified harms be ones that "could" rather than "would" occur, expanding the definition of "confidential sources," presuming that any information provided by a confidential source might identify the source, and expanding the number of documents that might be considered to cause damage to law enforcement investigative techniques, and expanding the exemption to cover the life or safety of any person.

(2) Definition of "Law Enforcement Purposes"

The term "law enforcement purposes" has been defined to include not only criminal enforcement purposes, but also civil and administrative enforcement.

j. Financial Institution Records and Oil Well Data

FOIA also protects records obtained from financial institutions, as well as oil well data, which the government collects in the course of its regulatory functions. The purpose of this exemption is to protect the institutions from which the data is collected, as well as to protect the government's ability to obtain the information.

k. Other Statutes That Preclude Disclosure

In addition to the FOIA exemptions, other federal statutes also specifically exempt documents from disclosure under FOIA. See, e.g., 21 U.S.C. § 1904(e)(3) (exempting information obtained or created in implementing the Foreign Narcotics Kingpin Designation Act, 21 U.S.C. §§ 1901–1908).

4. FOIA Time Limits

FOIA requires an administrative agency to decide within 20 working days whether to comply with a FOIA request. *See* 5 U.S.C.A. § 552(a)(6)(A)(i). If the agency decides to deny the request, it must do two things: explain the basis for its denial and inform the person of internal appeal opportunities. If the person chooses to appeal, the agency must decide the appeal within ten working days. In "unusual circumstances," such as when the facility containing the records is in a separate location from the agency's FOIA office, an agency may extend both of these deadlines for up to ten days. 5 U.S.C.A. § 552(a)(6)(B)(i).

a. Judicial Enforcement

Only rarely do agencies actually meet FOIA's time deadlines. When an agency does fail to meet a deadline, the requesting party may seek judicial review. 5 U.S.C.A. § 552(a)(6)(C). However, although a reviewing court should order immediate compliance absent "exceptional circumstances," most courts are patient provided that the agency can demonstrate that it is proceeding diligently.

b. The 1996 Amendments

In 1996, Congress amended FOIA to allow agencies to engage in variable processing of requests. In other words, agencies may process easier requests more quickly than more difficult requests, and may give priority to urgent requests. The Amendments also provide that, if an agency receives a very large request that cannot be expeditiously processed, it may notify the requester and give him/her an opportunity to narrow the request. If the requestor refuses, this fact can be treated as an "exceptional circumstance" for purposes of deciding whether the agency is entitled to extra time. Finally, the Amendments preclude a determination that "exceptional circumstances" exist if the delay results from a "predictable agency workload of requests," unless the agency is making "reasonable progress in reducing its backlog of pending requests."

5. FOIA Fees

The original FOIA authorized agencies to impose "fair and equitable charges" for processing requests. In 1974, Congress limited the ability of agencies to impose fees fearing that the fees would deter FOIA requests. Twelve years later, following a significant increase in the number of requests, Congress allowed agencies to recover the direct costs of search, duplication, and review associated with commercial requests. 5 U.S.C.A. § 552(a)(4)(A).

a. The Definition of "Review Costs"

Agencies may not charge requesters for amounts expended in "resolving issues of law or policy." In other words, if the agency is deciding whether to withhold documents under a FOIA privilege, they may not charge for that effort.

b. Waiver of Fees

Although agencies may charge commercial entities for producing documents, FOIA allows for a waiver of costs when "disclosure of the information is in the public interest because it is likely to contribute significantly to public understanding of the operations or activities of the government and is not primarily in the commercial interest of the requester." In addition, agencies may not charge for the first two hours of search time and the first 100 pages of duplication for any noncommercial request, and they also may not charge when the cost of collecting the fee would exceed the amount of the fee.

6. Judicial Review

When a FOIA request is denied, the requester may seek judicial review and the burden of proof rests upon the agency that is resisting disclosure. 5 U.S.C.A. § 552(a)(4)(B). Judicial review is *de novo* and the requester may recover reasonable attorney's fees and costs if he/she prevails. In addition, if the court believes that the agency acted arbitrarily or capriciously in denying the request, it may issue a written finding to that effect, thereby referring the matter to the Special Counsel of the Merit System Protection Board for disciplinary action. 5 U.S.C.A. § 552(a)(4)(F).

7. Justice Department Memoranda

Although the Justice Department (DOJ) represents administrative agencies in FOIA litigation, it may refuse to defend an agency when it believes that the agency's position is not supported by the facts or the law. In 1977, an Attorney General's memorandum stated that, even though agency records may technically be covered by a FOIA exemption, DOJ will not defend a refusal to disclose except when the release would be contrary to the public interest. Although President Reagan's Attorney General rescinded the 1977 memorandum, President Clinton's Attorney General Janet Reno issued a new memorandum, similar to the original one. Following the 9/11 attacks, Attorney General Ashcroft rescinded the Reno memorandum.

8. Reverse FOIA Actions

Sometimes, when agencies are asked to disclose information regarding an individual or company that would otherwise be exempt, the individual or company may sue to prevent disclosure. Such suits are referred to as "reverse FOIA actions."

a. Executive Order 12600

Executive Order 12600 establishes rules requiring predisclosure notification to affected individuals or companies before their confidential information is released. The order requires agencies to "establish procedures to permit submitters of confidential commercial information to designate, at the time the information is submitted to the Federal government or a reasonable time thereafter, any information the disclosure of which the submitter claims could reasonably be expected to cause substantial competitive harm." In addition, the order provides that the "head of each Executive department or agency shall, to the extent permitted by law, provide the submitter notice in accordance with section 1 of this Order whenever the department or agency determines that it may be required to disclose records." In addition, the EO allows the submitter to object to disclosure.

b. *Chrysler Corp. v. Brown*

In *Chrysler Corp. v. Brown*, 441 U.S. 281, 99 S.Ct. 1705, 60 L.Ed.2d 208 (1979), the Court held that FOIA is a disclosure statute and that Chrysler could not preclude disclosure of information under a suit brought under that statute. However, Chrysler also premised its suit on the Trade Secrets Act, 18 U.S.C. § 1905, which prohibits disclosure of trade secrets. The Court rejected Chrysler's contention "that the Trade Secrets Act affords a private right of action to enjoin disclosure in violation of the statute." However, the Court also held that it could seek review of the agency's disclosure decision as a "person suffering legal wrong because of agency action, or adversely affected or aggrieved by agency action . .

. [who] is entitled to judicial review thereof." 5 U.S.C. § 702. FOIA disclosure decisions are reviewed *de novo*.

F. THE FEDERAL ADVISORY COMMITTEE ACT

The Federal Advisory Committee Act (FACA), 5 U.S.C.A. §§ 1–15, regulates the use of advisory committees. FACA provides for monitoring the quantity of advisory committees and the amount of money spent by them. In addition, FACA prohibits the establishment of a new advisory committee, not established by the President or by statute, unless the head of the creating agency determines "as a matter of formal record . . . [that such establishment is] in the public interest in connection with the performance of duties imposed on that agency by law."

1. Procedural Requirements for the Creation of New Advisory Committees

FACA provides that any new advisory committee cannot meet until its "charter" has been filed in a number of places: with the Administrator for Presidential advisory committees, or the head of the agency to which the committee will report, and with designated committees in the House and Senate. The "charter" must contain various types of information (e.g., the committee's title, purpose, duration, etc.). FACA also limits advisory committees to two-years duration, but allows for extensions.

2. Requirement of Fairness and Balance

FACA requires that the membership of advisory committees be "fairly balanced in terms of the points of view represented and the functions to be performed by the advisory committee." In other words, committees may not be stacked to favor particular perspectives.

3. Governmental Participation and Involvement

FACA also provides that an advisory committee meeting may not take place "except with the approval of, or with the advance approval of, a designated officer or employee of the Federal Government, and [except for Presidential advisory committees] with an agenda approved by such officer or employee." In addition, a designated federal officer or employee must be present at the meeting, and the officer or employee is authorized to adjourn the meeting at any time "he determines it to be in the public interest."

4. FACA and Openness

FACA requires that "[e]ach advisory committee meeting shall be open to the public," and requires that "timely notice" of such meeting shall be published in the *Federal Register*. FACA also allows the public to appear and file statements with the committee, and requires committees to keep "detailed minutes of each meeting," the accuracy of which the chair of the committee must certify, and which must contain "a record of the persons present, a complete and accurate description of the matter discussed and conclusions reached, and copies of all reports received, issued, or approved by the advisory committee." These records must be available for public inspection and copying.

5. The *Public Citizen* Case

In *Public Citizen v. U.S. Department of Justice*, 491 U.S. 440, 109 S.Ct. 2558, 105 L.Ed.2d 377 (1989), the Court was asked to decide whether an American Bar Association committee that advised the Justice Department on judicial nominations was subject to FACA. The Court held that it was not and that FACA was not intended to apply to such advice.

6. FACA Enforcement

When FACA applies, but its provisions have not been satisfied, courts may (and often do) prohibit agencies from using information or recommendations derived from such committees.

G. GOVERNMENT IN THE SUNSHINE ACT

The Government in the Sunshine Act, 5 U.S.C.A. § 552b, requires that "every portion of every meeting of an agency shall be open to public observation." 5 U.S.C.A. § 552b(b).

1. Definition of "Agency"

Unlike FOIA, the Sunshine Act only applies to agencies "headed by a collegial body composed of two or more individual members, a majority of whom are appointed to such position by the President with the advice and consent of the Senate, and any subdivision thereof authorized to act on behalf of the agency." 5 U.S.C.A. § 552b(a)(1). In other words, it applies to agencies like the SEC, FTC, FCC, FEC, and other similar agencies headed by collegial bodies, but does not apply to cabinet level agencies.

2. Definition of "Meeting"

The Sunshine Act only applies when there is a meeting of a quorum of the members of the agency, and only when they are involved in "deliberations" that "determine or result in the joint conduct or disposition of official agency business." 5 U.S.C.A. § 552b(a)(2).

3. Exceptions

The Sunshine Act provides for closed meetings in certain specified situations, including meetings involving national defense and classified information, internal personnel rules, matters specifically exempted by statute, trade secrets and privileged or confidential commercial or financial information, information that would invade a person's privacy, investigatory records compiled for law enforcement purposes, and information related to reports prepared by or for an agency regulating financial institutions. 5 U.S.C.A. § 552b(c)(1)–(4), (6)–(8). The Act also contains exemptions for "accusing any person of a crime, or formally censuring any person;" for agencies regulating currencies, securities, or commodities, information the disclosure of which would likely lead to significant financial speculation or significantly endanger the stability of any financial institution, or in the case of any agency, information the disclosure of which would be likely to significantly frustrate implementation of a proposed agency action; and for information relating to an agency's issuance of a subpoena, participation in a civil action, or the conduct of a formal agency adjudication. 5 U.S.C.A. § 552b(c)(5), (9), (10).

4. Notice Requirement

The Sunshine Act mandates that agencies provide at least seven-days notice of a meeting's subject matter, time, place, and whether the meeting will be open or closed. 5 U.S.C.A. § 552b(e)(1). The Act also requires that the notice be published in the *Federal Register*, and that agencies maintain minutes or transcripts of all meetings, open or closed. 5 U.S.C.A. § 552b(f)(1).

5. Judicial Review

The Sunshine Act's provisions are judicially enforceable and the agency is required to justify its actions. 5 U.S.C.A. § 552b(h). A plaintiff may be entitled to recover attorney's fees and litigation costs in an enforcement action, but the Act does not permit a court to invalidate agency action taken in violation of the Sunshine Act. 5 U.S.C.A. § 552b(h)(2) ("Nothing in this section authorizes any Federal court having jurisdiction solely on the basis of paragraph (1) [of this subsection] to set aside, enjoin, or invalidate any agency action (other than an action to close a meeting or to withhold information under this section) taken or discussed at any agency meeting out of which the violation of this section arose.").

TRUE–FALSE QUESTIONS

1. FOIA is designed to protect governmental documents and information against unauthorized disclosure.

2. When an agency seeks to prevent disclosure of documents under FOIA, it bears the burden of proof.

3. In reviewing an agency's assertion of an exemption under FOIA, a reviewing court should be deferential to the agency's conclusions.

4. FOIA does not allow administrative agencies to charge for producing information.

5. FOIA requires administrative agencies to make an initial decision on FOIA requests within twenty days.

6. When an agency asserts FOIA exemptions, it is required to prepare a so-called "*Vaughn* Index," which has the effect of conclusively vindicating the exemption.

7. FACA requires that advisory committee meetings be open to the public.

8. FACA's requirements are judicially enforceable.

9. The Government in the Sunshine Act applies to all administrative agencies.

10. When an agency conducts a meeting in violation of the Government in the Sunshine Act, any actions taken at that meeting are invalid and will be enjoined by court order.

MULTIPLE CHOICE QUESTIONS

1. Which of the following exemptions is recognized under FOIA:

    A. Internal agency personnel rules and practices;

    B. Information specifically exempted from disclosure by statute;

    C. Inter-agency or intra-agency privileged communications;

    D. All of the above.

2. The Government in the Sunshine Act contains which of the following provisions:

    A. Agencies must publish, in the *Federal Register*, at least seven days in advance, a meeting's subject matter, time, and place.

    B. Agencies must publish, in the *Federal Register*, minutes of all their meetings.

C. Agencies are prohibited from holding closed meetings.

D. All of the above.

3. FACA prohibits which of the following:

A. The creation of new advisory committees not approved by Congress;

B. The creation of new advisory committees not approved by the President;

C. Advisory committees which are not "fairly balanced" in terms of their composition;

D. Advisory committees that remain in existence for more than three years without an extension.

ESSAY QUESTIONS

1. James Johnson files a FOIA request with the United States Department of Defense (DoD) seeking internal documents relating to the initiation of the Iraq War. DoD produces documents that were previously made public, but refuses to produce classified documents (particularly national security documents) relating to the initiation of the war. DoD asserts that all of the classified documents are highly confidential and it refuses to produce any information regarding those documents. You are the judge assigned to hear the case. What can you do to evaluate DoD's claim?

2. Your client contacts you with information that the Federal Internet Advisory Committee, established to advise the Federal Communications Commission regarding the Internet, has been holding secret deliberative meetings. Your client, who is an Internet service provider, asks you to take immediate action to protect its interests. What can or should you do?

3. Your client informs you that the Federal Internet Commission, a collegial body created to regulate the Internet, has been holding secret deliberative meetings. Your client, who is an Internet service provider, asks you to take immediate action. What should you do?

ANSWERS TO TRUE–FALSE QUESTIONS

1. False. FOIA is regarded as a "disclosure" statute, and is not designed to protect governmental documents and information against unauthorized disclosure.

2. True. When an agency seeks to prevent disclosure of documents under FOIA, it bears the burden of proof.

3. False. In reviewing an agency's assertion of an exemption under FOIA, a reviewing court acts *de novo*.

4. False. FOIA permits administrative agencies to charge for producing information in some situations. However, in some instances, FOIA disclosure fees can be waived.

5. True. FOIA requires administrative agencies to make an initial decision on FOIA requests within twenty days. However, courts are often patient if an agency does not meet this deadline.

6. False. When an agency asserts FOIA exemptions, it is required to prepare a so-called "*Vaughn* Index." However, the purpose of the index is to allow the claimant to challenge the agency's refusal to disclose.

7. True. FACA requires that advisory committee meetings be open to the public.

8. True. FACA's requirements are judicially enforceable.

9. False. The Government in the Sunshine Act does not apply to all administrative agencies. Rather, it applies only to collegial bodies.

10. False. When an agency conducts a meeting in violation of the Government in the Sunshine Act, courts are not authorized to invalidate or enjoin actions taken at the meeting.

ANSWERS TO MULTIPLE CHOICE QUESTIONS

1. Answer (D) is correct. All of the exemptions stated in answers (A)–(C) are proper FOIA exemptions. Thus, answer (D)'s "all of the above" is the correct answer.

2. Answer (A) is correct because the Government in the Sunshine Act requires agencies to publish, in the *Federal Register*, at least seven days in advance, a meeting's subject matter, time, and place. Answer (B) is incorrect because the

Act does not require agencies to publish, in the *Federal Register*, minutes of all their meetings. Answer (C) is incorrect because although the Act generally prohibits closed meetings, it does not always prohibit closure. Answer (D), "all of the above," is incorrect because answers (B) and (C) are incorrect.

3.   Answer (C) is correct because FACA prohibits advisory committees which are not fair and balanced. Answer (A) is incorrect because, although Congress has the authority to approve new advisory committees, approval can also come from the President or the head of the agency. Answer (B) is incorrect because, although the President can approve new advisory committees, they can also be approved by Congress or the head of the agency. Answer (D) is incorrect because advisory committees are term limited at two years, not three years, absent an extension.

ANSWERS TO ESSAY QUESTIONS

1.   If the documents are, in fact classified national security documents, DoD does not have to disclose them. However, at the very least, DoD must prepare a *Vaughn* Index in which it describes the documents and states why they are not subject to disclosure. In an appropriate case, the Court might even require an *in camera* inspection to ensure that the documents were properly classified under the agency's classification order. However, if the documents were properly classified, the court should not second-guess the classification order itself. Of course, a *Vaughn* Index might be dispensed with if disclosure of the document's existence will compromise security.

2.   Under FACA, "[e]ach advisory committee meeting shall be open to the public," and "timely notice" of each meeting shall be published in the *Federal Register*. As a result, this advisory committee is meeting in violation of FACA. Since FACA's provisions are judicially enforceable, it is possible to seek injunctive relief preventing adoption of the committee's recommendations.

3.   Under the Government in the Sunshine Act, an interested party cannot prohibit agency action from taking effect even if it was taken in violation of the Act. However, you can bring action to enforce the Sunshine Act's openness requirements, and the Act provides for attorney's fees and litigation expenses.

CHAPTER EIGHT

Attorney's Fees

A. GENERAL RULE: EACH SIDE BEARS ITS OWN COSTS

Under the so-called "American Rule," each side generally bears its own legal costs. However, statutes sometimes alter this rule.

B. EQUAL ACCESS TO JUSTICE ACT (EAJA) ALLOWS SOME FEE RECOVERY

The EAJA provides for a private party to collect attorney's fees when litigating against the government when certain conditions are met.

1. The Private Party Must Have Prevailed

Under the EAJA a "prevailing party" may collect reasonable attorney's fees from the government in an adversary proceeding. This rule does not apply if the adjudicative officer of the agency finds that the agency position was "substantially justified" or that special circumstances would render a fees award unjust.

2. Prevailing Status Is Determined Based on the Administrative Record

Whether the agency's position was "substantially justified" is to be determined based on the record of the administrative proceeding. 5 U.S.C. § 504.

3. Award May Be Limited if the Private Party Unreasonably Protracted the Proceedings

According to 5 U.S.C. § 504(a)(3), "The adjudicative officer of the agency may reduce the amount to be awarded, or deny an award, to the extent that the party during the course of the proceedings engaged in conduct which unduly and unreasonably protracted the final resolution of the matter in controversy."

4. Fees Available Against Excessive Demands

Fees are also available "if the demand by the agency is substantially in excess of the decision of the adjudicative officer and is unreasonable when compared with such decision." In such cases the party may recover fees and other expenses related to defending against the excessive demand. 5 U.S.C. § 504(a)(4).

5. Excessive Demand Fees Unavailable for Willful Violations or Bad Faith

Excessive demand fees are unavailable "if the party has committed a willful violation of law or otherwise acted in bad faith, or special circumstances make an award unjust." 5 U.S.C. § 504(a)(4).

6. Fees Include Witness Fees and Report Preparation

Under the EAJA fees include witness fees and report preparations. However, there are caps to the hourly rates at which fees and expenses may be recovered.

7. Prevailing Parties Limited by Size and Wealth

The EAJA defines "party" as individuals with a net worth of less than $2,000,000 and business associations with a net worth of less than $7,000,000 and less than 500 employees. These restrictions do not apply to tax-exempt parties.

8. Adversary Adjudication Includes Formal Adjudications

Under the EAJA an "adversarial adjudication" is an adjudication under 5 U.S.C. § 554—that is, a formal, on the record adjudication.

9. Voluntary Agency Provision of Formal Proceedings Does Not Trigger the EAJA

The EAJA applies only to adjudications where Congress intended it to apply. Thus, voluntary agency provision of a formal proceeding does not trigger its provisions.

10. Partial Prevailing Entitles Party to Some Fees

A party need not prevail entirely in order to claim at least some attorney's fees. A party receiving only a partial judgment may recover a proportionate fee award.

11. A Party May "Prevail" in the Absence of a Final Decision

Even without a final decision a party may still claim attorney's fees if it is able to show that the agency changed its position vis-à-vis the party, and that the adjudication was a substantial factor in that change.

12. Government's Justification Must Be Substantial

In order to avoid EAJA fees, the government must show that its position was "substantially justified." This requires simply that the position was justified to a point that would satisfy a reasonable person. However, in order to satisfy the requirement the government's position must be stronger than simply not meriting sanctions for frivolousness.

13. Government Position May Be Partially Justified

Some of the government's positions may be substantially justified while others may not. In such a situation partial fees are appropriate.

TRUE–FALSE QUESTIONS

1. The "substantially justified" standard has been understood to mean the standard that would apply when a court determines if a litigant is offering a frivolous argument.

2. Any private party may recover under the EAJA.

3. Under the American Rule the presumption is that victorious parties can obtain attorney's fees.

4. If the private party is found liable, it may still recover some fees if the agency's demands are deemed excessive.

5. Only attorney's fees, not witness or other expenses, are recoverable under the EAJA.

6. Attorney's fees are available under the EAJA only when Congress requires the agency to follow a formal adjudication procedure.

7. A case must proceed to a final judgment before attorney's fees may be awarded.

8. Awards under the EAJA may be denied if the party needlessly protracts the litigation.

MULTIPLE CHOICE QUESTION

Under which of the following scenarios would a prevailing party be most likely NOT to recover an award under the EAJA?

A. The case had not proceeded to final judgment, when the agency decided to change its policy toward the party, in the party's favor.

B.   The private party was found liable for violating the statute, but the agency had demanded a fine that was clearly excessive.

C.   The adjudication was the result of a formal proceeding that the agency was not required to provide the party.

D.   The agency lost, and no reasonable person could have thought the agency was correct on the key issues of law and fact.

ESSAY QUESTION

You have just discovered that your client has prevailed in an adjudication against an agency. What information would you need in order to determine whether your client would be eligible for any attorney fee recovery under the EAJA?

ANSWERS TO TRUE–FALSE QUESTIONS

1.   False.   The "substantially justified" standard requires a stronger showing than that simply needed to avoid sanctions for frivolous litigation.

2.   False.   The EAJA sets forth net worth and corporate size ceilings for eligible parties.

3.   False.   Under the American Rule each side is responsible for its own costs.

4.   True.   The EAJA provides for fee recovery for excessive rewards, absent willful violation or bad faith by the private party.

5.   False.   The EAJA allows recovery of witness fees and expenses such as the preparation of reports.

6.   True.   If the agency voluntarily provides a formal process, the EAJA does not apply.

7.   False.   The EAJA provides for attorney's fees in cases that stop short of final judgment.

8.   True.   The EAJA allows this restriction on a party's fee recovery.

ANSWER TO MULTIPLE CHOICE QUESTION

The correct answer is (C). The EAJA applies only when Congress intends it to provide. Normally this means that it applies only when the agency is required by statute to engage in a formal adjudication. The fact that the agency provided such a proceeding of its own grace does not bring it within the ambit of the EAJA. (A) is incorrect because the EAJA provides for fees even when the case has not proceeded to final judgment. (B) is incorrect because fees can be recovered for defending against excessive agency demands, even if the private party violated the statute or regulation at issue in the case. (D) is incorrect because if no reasonable person could have thought the agency had the better argument then fee recovery would be allowed.

ANSWER TO ESSAY QUESTION

You would need to know at least the following: (1) was the agency's position substantially justified; (2) did you client engage in any dilatory tactics; (3) was the proceeding required by statute to be a formal adjudication; and (4) did your client have a net worth (or if a business association, did it employ a sufficiently large number of people) as to take it out of the EAJA's coverage.

Table of Cases

Index

✝